Hodder Gibson

Scottish Examination Materials

HIGHER
ENGLISH
Close Reading

Ann Bridges *and* Colin Eckford

Hodder Gibson

A MEMBER OF THE HODDER HEADLINE GROUP

The Publishers would like to thank the following for permission to reproduce copyright material:

Photo credits page 91 © iStockphoto.com/Andres Rodriguez; page 121 © iStockphoto.com/Slavoljub Pantelic

Acknowledgements Extract from 'We have mutated into a surveillance society – and must share the blame' by Jonathan Raban, copyright Guardian Newspapers Limited 2006; Extract from 'Mr Blobby' by Jon Richfield, from *Does Anything Eat Wasps,* published by Profile Books; Extract from 'With junk food or with no food, we are killing our children without objection' by Ian Bell, reproduced with the permission of The Herald and Sunday Herald © Newsquest (Herald and Times) Ltd; Extract from 'Sinking London' by Hillary Shaw, from *Does Anything Eat Wasps,* published by Profile Books; Extract from *Clean and Decent: The fascinating history of the bathroom and the water closet, and of sundry habits, fashions and accessories of the toilet principally in Great Britain, France and America* by Lawrence Wright, published by Routledge/Taylor & Francis, 1960; Extract from 'An eye for an eye' by Ian Bell, reproduced with the permission of The Herald and Sunday Herald © Newsquest (Herald and Times) Ltd; Extract from 'A classroom with a view' by Jonathan Glancey, copyright Guardian Newspapers Limited 2006; Extract from 'Glamour Women of the Year Awards' by Sylvia Patterson, reproduced with the permission of The Herald and Sunday Herald © Newsquest (Herald and Times) Ltd; Extract from 'Not in my manor' by Will Self, copyright Guardian Newspapers Limited 2006; Extract from 'The secret life of handbags' by Jeremy Clarkson, reproduced with permission of *The Sunday Times*; Extract from 'The depressing reality of jury service' by Matthew Lewin, copyright *The Independent*, 4th February 2004; Extract from 'Serving on a jury restored my faith in humanity' by Mark Steel, copyright *The Independent*, 12th February 2004; Extract from 'In praise of the lowly teenager' by Kate Figes, published in *The Times*, 10th May 2004, reproduced by permission of the author; Extract from 'Let's make the young lead the way' by Jackie Kemp, published in *The Herald*, 29th May 2002, reproduced by permission of the author; Extract from 'Put the fear of God into these thugs' by Jenny McCartney, reproduced by permission of *The Telegraph*; Extract from 'Once Upon a Time We Read Our Children Stories' by Michael Morpurgo, published in *The Times*, 3rd March 2005; Extract from 'Thou shalt read' by Anthony Horowitz, reproduced by permission of *The Telegraph*; 'The cheapening of grief', extracted from 'How we wallow in our selective grief', by Katie Grant, published in *The Scotsman*, 11th October 2004, reproduced by permission of the author; 'Why this parade of grief', extracted from 'This circus of grief has nothing to do with Best' by Peter Preston, copyright Guardian Newspapers Limited 2005; Extract from 'Sports days when losing is a winner' by Jackie Kemp, published in *The Herald*, 4th June 2003, reproduced by permission of the author; Extract from 'Training ground for no-goals mediocrity' by Gillian Bowditch, reproduced by permission of The Scotsman Publications Limited; Extract from 'The girls can't help it' by Jenny McCartney, reproduced by permission of *The Telegraph*; Extract from 'The Fight To Save Our Food' by Colin Tudge, reproduced with the permission of The Herald and Sunday Herald © Newsquest (Herald and Times) Ltd; Extract from 'I'm lovin' it' by High Fearnley-Whittingstall, copyright Guardian Newspapers Limited 2006; '"Weirdness Dust" No More', extracted from 'Why young adults are happy to stay at home' by Melanie Reid, reproduced with the permission of The Herald and Sunday Herald © Newsquest (Herald and Times) Ltd; Extract from 'The war of the generations may soon be over' by Deborah Orr, copyright *The Independent*, 22nd October 2002; Extract from 'Taking politicians at their words' by Barry Didcock, reproduced with the permission of The Herald and Sunday Herald © Newsquest (Herald and Times) Ltd; Extract from 'Weasel words and forked tongues' by Rafael Behr, copyright Guardian Newspapers Limited 2006; Extract from 'Blame the Victorians for our migraines and divorces' by Madeleine Bunting, copyright Guardian Newspapers Limited 2003; Extract from 'What are you planning on doing for Christmas?' by Terence Blacker, copyright *The Independent*, 18th October 2002; Extract from *Mountains of the Mind* by Robert McFarlane is reprinted by permission of Granta Publications.

The authors would like to thank the English Department at Madras College and also Bill Marshall for their help during the preparation of this book.

Every effort has been made to trace all copyright holders, but if any have been inadvertently overlooked the Publishers will be pleased to make the necessary arrangements at the first opportunity.

Although every effort has been made to ensure that website addresses are correct at time of going to press, Hodder Gibson cannot be held responsible for the content of any website mentioned in this book. It is sometimes possible to find a relocated web page by typing in the address of the home page for a website in the URL window of your browser.

Hachette's policy is to use papers that are natural, renewable and recyclable products and made from wood grown in sustainable forests. The logging and manufacturing processes are expected to conform to the environmental regulations of the country of origin.

Orders: please contact Bookpoint Ltd, 130 Milton Park, Abingdon, Oxon OX14 4SB. Telephone: (44) 01235 827720. Fax: (44) 01235 400454. Lines are open 9.00 – 5.00, Monday to Saturday, with a 24-hour message answering service. Visit our website at www.hoddereducation.co.uk. Hodder Gibson can be contacted direct on: Tel: 0141 848 1609; Fax: 0141 889 6315; email: hoddergibson@hodder.co.uk

© Ann Bridges and Colin Eckford 2007
First published in 2007 by
Hodder Gibson, an imprint of Hodder Education,
part of Hachette Livre UK,
2a Christie Street
Paisley PA1 1NB

Impression number   5 4
Year   2010 2009 2008

Cover photo © Image Source/Alamy
Typeset in Garamond 11pt by Fakenham Photosetting Limited, Fakenham, Norfolk
Printed in Great Britain by Martins the Printers, Berwick upon Tweed.

A catalogue record for this title is available from the British Library

ISBN: 978-0-340-92808-0

Contents

Introduction

Why is close reading tested at all? Faced with the intricacies of Marking Schemes and the proliferation of questions and codes, it is a question which might be asked – and not just by the students.

The first reason can be found in the passages and extracts students are expected to be able to read and understand. These are non-fiction passages designed for an adult readership. The topics vary but the reading usually involves students in confronting ideas and opinions about issues of the day. If nothing else they will become better informed about society and its concerns.

The concentration on non-fiction is an antidote to the more literary studies which students undertake. Despite the expansion of opportunities in the Higher English course to read non-fiction texts in a critical way, there has not been a similar expansion of such texts studied. As a considerable proportion of an educated adult's reading is likely to be non-fiction – newspapers, work related documents, books on leisure pursuits and interests, for example – it seems self-evident that students should be practising the skill of reading these texts in school or college.

In such writing the level of vocabulary and the complexity of sentence structure can act as a barrier to the simple understanding of these texts, so that presenting such passages for close reading will, in time, develop the student's ability to read for information.

However, that is not enough in a world where almost no text is neutral. There is a series of devices commonly used which create bias, 'spin', enthusiasm and entertainment. The ability to spot and analyse these devices allows the reader to be critical, to appreciate at a more subtle level the communications which come her way. Not only will the reading experience become richer, the reader will be better equipped to take an active part in debate and in the democratic process.

That takes care of understanding and analysis. The evaluative process is one which follows the previous two in that it becomes second nature to reflect on a piece just read and see where it has left one's views, one's knowledge and, occasionally, one's temper.

This book is designed to help with the detailed study of close reading in the way that it is dealt with at Higher level in English, but the overarching idea should not be lost sight of. There are many small trees, but the important feature is the wood.

The first Part of the book uses short passages, each of which concentrates on developing understanding and the ability to comment on one of the techniques commonly adopted by writers of non-fiction. Of course there is overlap among the techniques of all these passages, just as there is an overlap between understanding and analysis and between analysis and evaluation. The topics are as varied as handbags, DIY, and the Olympics. There are a number of exercises associated with each passage, the answers to which come at the end of the Part.

The second Part of the book consists of passages for comparison. These are longer and concentrated more on issues which create debate. Examples of topics are the strengths and weaknesses of the jury system, and the exploration of public grief and its manipulation by the media. These passages give opportunities for discussion, summary and comparison. There are associated exercises, the answers to which can be found in the separate Answers and Marking Schemes book.

The last Part of the book consists of six double passages for practice in close reading, formatted as in the Higher examination. The topics include Teenage Magazines, Mountaineering and Christmas. There are extensive and detailed Marking Instructions for each passage which are also found in the separate Answers and Marking Schemes book.

The materials in the first two Parts provide alternatives to the practice of churning through complete past papers; they can provide a teaching focus or a remedial focus on individual aspects of close reading skills. The third section provides ample practice for the run up to prelims or to the examination.

Over and above all this, the practice of reading topical passages, and spotting the interesting ways in which the subjects are presented, should lead on to further reading and analysis. Students should be encouraged to find interesting short extracts which can be the subject of a ten minute discussion, or a short written exercise on a particular technique. In this way a number of topics and techniques can be dealt with fairly briefly in a stimulating way (or before everyone gets bored stiff). The real objective at the end of a Higher English course should not just be an examination pass, but a mature and interested approach to reading in all its forms.

Part One
Concepts

Part One

Introduction

The articles on which the exercises in this Part of the book depend have been chosen to illustrate various aspects and techniques associated with close reading. Each chapter contains a topical article or an extract from a book. The typical structure starts with a brief introduction to the specified technique followed by the article. Next there is a series of points to consider, which give advice and exemplification based on the article. There are tasks to be performed, and at the end there is a reminder of the technical terminology which has been illustrated in the course of the chapter or in the associated answers. The exercises for further practice could be used either for consolidation or for revision purposes at a later date.

The answers to the questions are at the end of this Part. The answers are very full – sometimes seeming to verge on the indulgent. They are not the answers which will typically have been produced by the average Higher candidate (although there is proof that some candidates do produce answers which are as fully developed as any in these pages). The purpose of the answers is to cover a variety of possibilities which will help the readers to see beyond what they themselves have written and to be encouraged to think along the lines suggested by the answers. The answers are actually very important to the usefulness and scope of this part of the book. There is a wealth of detail and advice which is designed to complement the initial 'teaching' material in the body of the chapter. There are also, in some cases, commentaries on the answers which provide useful pointers of a general kind.

It cannot be emphasised too much that the answers are as important as a teaching and learning tool as the original exercises. Their usefulness is not for letting students 'mark' their own work – it is to see in practice the kinds of appropriate comments which are acceptable, and, by constantly being exposed to the terminology and formulae of such successful answers, to pick up good habits which will help them organise their thoughts.

Throughout these exercises and answers there is a wide range of complex vocabulary which may stretch the average student, but exposure to these words and concepts should extend her critical vocabulary. They also demonstrate the need for expansion of the active vocabulary available to provide the connotations, synonyms and 'translations' which are necessary to the effective answering of questions. Often students show in their answers that they have the right idea for an answer but they lack the vocabulary to express what they know. These exercises (and answers) may help a little, but the basic work has to be done by more and more reading of high level language. If the only non-fiction articles that are read by the students are the passages in this book and a sprinkling of past papers, then their chances of success are limited.

Word Choice

What is special about 'word choice' in the way that it is identified for questioning in Higher Close Reading passages? It is surely obvious that all professional writers do choose their words with care, so all words can be described as 'chosen'. However, by focusing on the use of particular words in particular contexts you can see how you are being manipulated, or entertained, or attracted, or emotionally affected by the writer's choice. In descriptive passages, word choice might be a main method whereby the mood or atmosphere of a particular scene is conveyed. In persuasive passages, word choice might be one of the methods used to influence your ideas, or predispose you to look on the argument favourably. In a piece of comic writing, the word choice will alert you to the tone and set up expectations for entertainment.

Given the nature of the kind of passages normally examined in Close Reading papers, it is more than likely that the main focus will be on words which attempt to influence you by conveying ideas from the writer's point of view. There will also be occasions when a descriptive passage or a humorous tone is marked by interesting and emotive word choice.

Denotation and Connotation

The effect of words on you, their ability to move you, or persuade you, depends on their connotations. All words have a denotation – a direct definition or basic 'meaning'.

> An infant, for example, is 'the young of the human species'.
> A baby is also 'the young of the human species'.
> And so is a 'neonate' – except that that's what they call them in hospital.

The connotations of these words are, however, very different.

'Infant' is a sort of social description – it marks out a small member of the human race; one of us, but very young (in its original Latin derivation it means 'not speaking').
'Baby' is a much more personal description suggesting affection, closeness, vulnerability.
'Neonate' is the medical description of a newly born child. It has connotations of classification, objectivity.

If the plight of these young beings in a refugee camp were being described there might be three separate descriptions which would have very different effects on you:

'Starving babies'
'Malnutrition among the infants'
'Neonatal death rate'.

Think about what these different effects are and what kind of communication you would be likely to find each in.

Word Choice (a) – persuasive

Often the words a writer uses are 'loaded' in such a way as to push you into accepting his or her **point of view**.

Exercise

The following article by Jonathan Raban in the Guardian *illustrates some of the ways in which this happens.*

He is writing about the 'surveillance' society – one in which we are all watched all the time, and may be watching others.

> 1   In the last few years, most of us - even instinctive technophobes like me - have become practised in the dark art of surveillance. When I'm going to meet a stranger at dinner, I'll routinely feed her name to Google and LexisNexis to find out who she is and what she's been up to lately. If you
> 5   know the person's street address, you can spy on her house with Google Earth, and inspect the state of her roof and how she keeps her garden. A slight tilt of camera angle, and you'd be able to see into her sock drawer and monitor the bottles in her liquor cabinet.
>   The seemingly bottomless capacity of the computer to store billions of
> 10 unrelated bits of information, and the extraordinary facility of search engines to trawl through the stuff, have made this kind of warrantless intrusion into other people's lives irresistible - to private individuals and to governments alike. We're all dataminers now. Just 10 or 15 years ago, it would have taken days in libraries and record offices, along with the full-time services of a
> 15 private detective, to get the kind of hard intelligence on my prospective dinner date that I can now retrieve in a few idle minutes; and if I can do that, I tremble to think of what governments, equipped with massive financial and technological resources, are capable of doing.
>   Last week, USA Today reported that the National Security Agency (the US
> 20 intelligence organisation so secretive that it's popularly known as the No Such Agency) is assembling 'the world's biggest database' of records of phone calls made within the United States since 2001. The NSA, it's said, is not listening to those calls, but is using them for 'social network analysis', looking for cluster patterns that might betray a terrorist cell. Exactly how, on
>
> ➤

25 this basis, one distinguishes a terrorist cell from a bridge club hasn't yet
been properly explained.

Of course, phone call monitoring is not the only weapon of surveillance.
Since September 11, CCTV cameras, magnetometers, BioWatch air-sniffers,
razor wire, concrete fortifications and all the rest of the machinery of state

30 security and surveillance have become so much a part of the furniture of
life in the US that we barely notice them. Year by year the government
grows more importunately parental, the citizenry more obediently childish.
Of course they log our phone calls – who are we to contradict the grown-
ups who wage their hi-tech secret war on our behalf? They know best.

35 There's obvious reason for alarm at these developments, in Britain as in
the US. But people cannot fairly expect their governments to observe higher
standards of delicacy and restraint than they demand of themselves. We're all
in this together. Almost overnight we've mutated into a surveillance society,
largely thanks to the Internet and its search engines.

40 Some weeks ago, I read in the New York Times that the western
headquarters of the No Such Agency is located somewhere to the northeast
of Yakima, in Washington state. I couldn't resist launching Google Earth and
visiting Yakima. Moving the cursor, clicking the mouse, I moved steadily
northeastward, into land marked 'Military Reservation'. There in the desolate

45 acres of sagebrush I came across what looked like an ailing mushroom farm
of scattered dome and dish antennae, and zoomed in. I found no secrets, but
the action supplied a neat image for these peculiar times: the surveilled
surveilling the surveiller who's surveilling him.

Points to consider

From the italicised introduction to the article, and from his description of surveillance
as a 'dark art' (line 2) with its implication of black magic, you get the impression that
the writer is suspicious of the merits of surveillance. If an article on this topic had
been written by a police spokesperson talking about the benefits to the public of
CCTV cameras, he or she would not have used the phrase 'dark art'.

Paragraph 1

Let's look at other words in this paragraph – first for their denotations and then for
their connotations.

Word	Denotation	Connotation
routinely	regularly	routinely also suggests something so mechanical that we no longer have to think about it. The moral implications of finding out about people's personal details no longer bother us
feed (her name)	put	in its original meaning this suggests being given up to be swallowed (by the machine) – fed to the lions – not a friendly act
spy	to watch, observe	spying has the added sinister connotations of illegal, covert activity
monitor	to watch, to check	there are also the critical connotations of monitor, where you are not only watching, but watching for wrong-doing (in this case probably the rate of consumption of alcohol)

In some of the answers given above, there is an implication that the **effect** of these connotations is to make the activity seem very suspect and intrusive. In most actual examination questions on word choice, however, you will be asked to go further and make explicit comment on the effect of the connotations, rather than simply to identify them.

Paragraph 2 (lines 9–18)
Keep this point in mind when considering the following words:

- bottomless
- trawl
- stuff
- warrantless
- intrusion
- dataminers
- hard (intelligence)
- idle
- tremble
- massive

Question

A For each of the words listed above give the denotation followed by the connotations of the word and also a **comment** on how these connotations keep pushing the writer's hostile point of view – that is, a comment on their **effect**.

Answer on page 53

Paragraph 3 (lines 19–26)

Up to this point we have considered the appropriateness of the connotations of words in suggesting or confirming Raban's point of view. But there are ways by which the basic connotations of the words can be extended, or altered, or intensified, or subverted.

The simple device of putting words in **inverted commas** causes the accepted meaning/implication of the words to be in some way subverted or queried.

'Social network analysis' is a good example of this.

Juxtaposition is another such device. It is the technique of putting words side by side to reinforce or conflict with each other. This often leads to an **incongruous** mismatch – which can have a comic effect. (There is more on this topic in Concept Seven – Exaggeration.)

A criticism of the surveillance jargon term 'cluster pattern' is given by two examples of a possible application, one appropriate and one inappropriate, and the simple juxtaposition of these two phrases triggers a sense of incongruity that makes for humour or satire:

'terrorist cell' and 'bridge club'.

Questions

B (a) What is the effect of putting the 'technical' phrase 'social network analysis' into inverted commas? (line 23)

(b) What does 'cluster pattern' mean in this context?

(c) What sinister connotations is Raban hinting at?

(d) Consider 'terrorist cell' and 'bridge club'. What are the associations of each of these?

(e) How does the juxtaposition work in ridiculing the attitude of the NSA?

Answers on page 54

Paragraph 4 (lines 27–34)

Here we find yet another series of devices which help the writer to promote his view of surveillance. There are interesting examples of word choice in the use of 'machinery' and 'furniture (of life)' which can be analysed in the normal denotation/connotation/effect pattern. However, in this paragraph the effect of his word choice is strengthened by its deployment in various structural devices.

Firstly the **list** (lines 28–29) juxtaposes at least three terms whose connotations clash so strongly that a vivid impression is quickly created that NSA cannot be taken seriously as an intelligent unit:

magnetometers   BioWatch air-sniffers   razor wire.

Secondly in line 32 the **parallel/balanced structure** contrasts 'importunately parental' against 'obediently childish'. The more formal, latinate word choice of the former carries with it the implication of intrusive, dictatorial demands; the more basic homely, ordinary word choice of the latter suggests or criticizes our supine compliance, especially 'childish'. 'Grown-ups' and 'they know best' obviously continue the parent–child analogy to confirm the impression.

Questions

C (a) What are the connotations and the effect of 'machinery' and 'furniture (of life)' on your view of this aspect of American society?

(b) What connotations, scientific or otherwise, are suggested to you by each of the three terms: 'magnetometers', 'BioWatch air-sniffers', 'razor wire'?

(c) What impression does the juxtaposition of these three terms give of the credibility of the NSA?

Answers on page 55

Paragraphs 5 and 6 (lines 35–48)

In these lines we find several words which are worth commenting on. The first of these is 'mutated' (line 38). The word means 'changed' but the connotations here are more of a sci-fi nature connected with transformations of species into alien or cloned or robotic creatures. These connotations suggest that mankind's 'progress' in hi-tech ability is detrimental to his humanity.

Question

D What effect does the word choice of 'Military Reservation', 'desolate acres' and 'ailing mushroom farm' have on your impression of the importance of the NSA?

Answer on page 55

Writer's Point of View

In the article we have just looked at, the writer's choice of words has the effect of encouraging you to believe in his view, that there is too much surveillance in society. No counterargument has been put forward at any point in the article, so it is up to the intelligent reader to recognise the article as a one-sided view of the topic.

Word Choice (b) – evocative/atmospheric

On other occasions, the writer's use of word choice is not to convey opinion or point of view but to share with you the feelings and atmosphere aroused by the description of, for example, a particular place. The following small extract from *The Wreckers* by Bella Bathurst gives an example of how the choice of words and the imagery suggest a very hostile place.

> 1   Up ahead there is nothing but the sea and an immense black semi-circle of rocks. These are not the softened, liquid-looking stones of the bay near St Mary's. These are savage-looking things, a giant hell-mouth ringed with black-tipped fangs. Any ship unwary enough to become entangled among them
> 5   would be sliced to splinters within seconds. Alongside the larger reefs, there are little ones poking only a few feet out of the water like archetypal sharks' fins, rocks with ridges so sharp you could slice meat with them, enormous squared-off lumps of granite, whole islands without a single horizontal surface. This is an Alcatraz, and these rocks are the everlasting version of
> 10   bullets and razor wire. The brassy light gives them all a strange burned beauty, and within that beauty, a deep sense of menace.

Points to consider

It is sometimes difficult to make an absolute distinction between word choice and imagery. Later on in this part of the book there is a detailed discussion of imagery. In all cases, however, the connotations of the words are all-important. In the following list there are many examples of word choice which use metaphorical connotations. When you are dealing with the denotation and connotations of words it is likely that you will naturally be alluding to the image contained in the word.

Questions

E   This first list of words, however, contains straightforward examples of atmospheric word choice. Show how effective each is in evoking the danger of the place.

- 'immense'
- 'enormous'
- 'squared-off'
- 'lumps'
- 'menace'

➤

F This next list of words, on the other hand, makes use of connotations which have metaphorical qualities. For example 'sliced' (line 5) – cut – has connotations which suggest how easily the wooden ship is damaged in several places as with a cleaver or knife cutting soft meat, not simply making one gash in the ship's side but an actual division of the ship into parts, which is more serious.

Try the following examples showing how they contribute to the sense of danger:

- 'softened, liquid-looking stones'
- 'splinters'
- 'brassy light'
- 'strange burned beauty'

Answers on page 56

The expressions in the list below are obviously examples of imagery and would be dealt with in the way suggested in Concept Five. The following question could be attempted now, or as a follow-on activity to Concept Five.

Question

G Show how the following examples of imagery create a vivid impression of the hostility of the scene:

- 'a giant hell mouth ringed with black-tipped fangs'
- 'like archetypal sharks' fins'
- 'so sharp you could slice meat'
- 'an Alcatraz'
- 'rocks are the everlasting version of bullets and razor wire'

Answers on page 57

List of terms used:

- **word choice**
- **denotation**
- **connotation**
- **juxtaposition**
- **list**
- **inverted commas**

- **point of view**
- **incongruity**
- **balance**
- **parallel**
- **contrast**
- **(extended) image**

Word Choice – further practice

This passage allows for further practice in writing about word choice for persuasive purposes. The passage is short and fairly straightforward but offers many opportunities to look at the connotative area of the writer's language.

Exercise

This article is from the magazine New Scientist.

Mr Blobby

1   Magazines are full of stories about cellulite and the many imaginative and expensive cures available. The question we have to ask ourselves is what is cellulite, and which cures work?

   Reputable scientific research seems to suggest that such miraculous
5   claims are characteristic of quackery, one of the biggest parasitic industries on the planet, ranking with politics, recreational drugs and bad-faith litigation. The word 'cellulite' was coined to exploit rich innocents. It has no clear definition, which is why quacks say so little about what it is.

   Cellulite amounts to subcutaneous fat tissue that has accumulated to the
10 point where it bulges between strands of connective tissue, forming an untidy grid like mud oozing through a duckboard. It is found mainly in people who are beyond their first youth, and getting rid of cellulite is just getting rid of fat.

   What makes cellulite so notorious is that it forms most offensively where
15 the body is least inclined to consume fat deposits, so reducing it takes persistent good dietary sense. No fancy exercise machine, flashy cream or black box changes that.

   For sound information about a large range of such subjects there are useful, factual, websites which perform an invaluable public service. Use
20 these websites and you will have an antidote to scare stories and a defence against medical fads and scams. Quacks and faddists hate, hate, hate them.

There are many examples in this article of emotive language being used to influence your opinion.

Questions

A Choose 10 words which suggest that, in the writer's view, the business made out of reducing cellulite is immoral and show how the connotations of these words are intended to influence you.

Normally, in answering such a question on the effect of the choice of words, you would move from the denotation, through the connotation to the comment which links with the question. Here, in this particular exercise, because all the words are chosen to reflect the same limited point of view, you are only required to look at denotation and connotation.

A typical comment in response to this question would probably be that the connotations of the word imply or suggest deception or exploitation. In the first example, which is done for you, the comment on the effect is added to show what would normally constitute a fully developed answer.

Word	Denotation	Connotation
imaginative	created in the mind	made up, fanciful, far fetched, ineffective

The **effect** is to suggest that the cures sold are worthless deceptions.

B Choose five words which suggest that there is reliable evidence to negate such fanciful claims and show how they create an impression of trustworthiness.

Answers on page 58

Sentence Structure

Sentences are the basic building blocks of our communication. They put words in sequences which make sense, and they communicate, for example, an instruction or an idea, or a question. Their shape can increase your understanding, your enjoyment and appreciation. The understanding of the effect of the structuring of a sentence is hard to explain. Most of us can see that there are tricks the writer has used to affect the way we read, but it is difficult to express how these tricks work. You can identify a number of signals that something special is happening, including: short sentences; repetition of clause, phrase, word or sound; parallelism of structure; balance; antithesis; climax; parenthesis; obvious punctuation marks. Merely identifying these features, however, will profit you nothing: you have to make a worthwhile comment about their effect.

Exercise

Look at the following article from a style magazine.

Decorating Should Come With a Health Warning

1 A mania has swept over the land. Our TVs, magazines and prized out-of-town wastelands have been given over to acres of blond-wood, angle-poised lamps and more MDF than you can shake a pulped stick at. Throughout the country, front rooms masquerading as 19th-century bordellos, Scandinavian
5 saunas and south-east Asian opium dens have been the disastrous result of this mental contagion.

   Though our society has an overabundance of information and material wealth, there's one thing we never have enough of – attention. Attention from friends who can't chat because they're on their way to Habitat;
10 attention from the boss who'd rather we kept to e-mail; attention from family who are always glued to Changing Rooms. So what better way to gain attention than by redesigning the living space as the set for our own very special movie?

   Some people say decoration is about having 'nice things' around you.
15 Nonsense. Home decoration is an ideology of personal transformation. If followed avidly, it ensures that the next time you have guests round, they'll either be stunned into silence or forced to gasp in admiration about your daring reinterpretation of the sixties, post-retro, plastic-flower explosion movement. Believe me, you'll be noticed.
20   Modern British telly bears the biggest responsibility for brainwashing us into believing a new front room equals a new outlook on life. Changing

➤

> Rooms, Tool Stories, Home Front, you know the drill: take three couples, shuffle them with an interior designer/DIY expert/measly budget, see what sticks. And if you thought we had reached saturation point, be warned,
> 25 more are on the way. Most prominently, To DIY For Better For Worse, in which a young couple moving in together are filmed arguing about which sofa to plump for.
>
> OK, we are all adults and can make our own life choices. Yes, we want ourselves and our families to be surrounded by nice objects that mark us
> 30 out as people of good taste, but don't take it to extremes. Lay down your nail-guns, good people.

Points to consider

You should have grasped the overall meaning of this article fairly quickly. The only sentence which could perhaps cause you trouble is in line 15: 'Home decoration is an ideology of personal transformation.' Perhaps by the time you have finished work on the sentence structure, the meaning will be clearer – or, perhaps not!

Short sentences
- 'A mania has swept over the land.' (line 1)
- 'Nonsense.' (line 15)
- 'Believe me, you'll be noticed.' (line 19)
- 'Lay down your nail-guns, good people.' (lines 30–31)

We could say of each of these, 'It is used for impact/emphasis.' Well, yes it is. But so is any short sentence in any article, in any book. As a comment, it may be correct, but it's not very sophisticated.

What we have to do is to see what particular impact each of these sentences has in its own context, because that context is unique. It's not just any short sentence, it's this short sentence, in this place, in this article.

'A mania has swept over the land.' This is not only the first sentence in its paragraph, and therefore likely to be the topic sentence of the paragraph, it is also the first sentence in the article, and indeed the topic sentence for the whole article. The fact that it is a short sentence lets the reader see very clearly that the important idea is 'mania'. It stands alone as a warning of what is to follow – a description of this mania. The idea of mania sweeping over the land, rather like a disease, also picks up a hint from the headline: 'Health Warning'. And it is given prominence through such brevity.

'Nonsense.' The first thing to notice is that this is a one word sentence, a 'minor sentence', if you want to call it that, a sentence which has no finite verb. It is worth identifying this fact, but, in itself, it is not enough – there needs to be more comment about what this particular sentence is doing at this point in the article. It stands between two statements: 'Some people say decoration is about having "nice things" around you' and 'Home decoration is an ideology of personal transformation.' It is obviously making you disagree with the first so that you can agree with the second. In other words it is very powerful in making you adopt the writer's view that home decoration is much more fundamental than simply having things look nice. It is blunt, dogmatic; it halts the reader in his tracks and pushes attention onto the following statement. (You may find that you now have a better idea about what 'Home decoration is an ideology of personal transformation' means.)

Questions

A (a) Explain the impact of the last sentence of paragraph 3 (line 19): 'Believe me, you'll be noticed'.

    (b) 'Lay down your nail guns, good people.' (lines 30–31) Show how this sentence contributes to the tone of the article and your appreciation of the writer's point of view.

Answers on page 61

Lists or series

One aspect of structure which is easy to identify is a 'list'. When you see a series of commas, or semi-colons, the temptation is to say something like 'the commas make up a list'. This is not true. Commas do not make a list. A number of items make a list, and the separation between these items is signalled by a comma or a semi-colon. As we have seen already, though, these comments could be made about any list, and what we are in the business of is providing specific comments about possible 'lists' in this article.

The most obvious one is in lines 8–11:

> Attention from friends who can't chat because they're on their way to Habitat; attention from the boss who'd rather we kept to e-mail; attention from family who are always glued to Changing Rooms.

The effect of this series of parallel climactic phrases is to provide the reader with information about the people who cannot provide what we want – attention. You could say that it shows the number of people who can't show attention and thus highlights the *scale* of the problem we are facing. Although this is possibly true here (and very often is in longer lists), it's more effective in this context in showing the *scope* of the lack of attention – from friends right down to family. It suggests that there is *nobody* to pay us any attention. You could also make the comment that the writer's line of thought is made clearer to you in this sentence because the semi-colons throw emphasis on each of the listed items making the reader give each his full attention. It also leaves you in no doubt about which group of people is being referred to in each part of the sentence.

Repetition

Before we leave this particular example, it is worth noting that part of the power of the sentence is achieved through the repetition of the word 'attention' right at the beginning of each phrase. But there is more to be said. The sentence preceding our example is:

> Though our society has an overabundance of information and material wealth, there's one thing we never have enough of – attention.

The function of the dash here is to set up the expectation that the answer to the question – 'what is "the one thing we never have enough of"' – will follow the dash. And the answer is 'attention'. Structurally, the idea of attention is being signalled for development. The fact that the first mention of 'attention' is after a dash, isolated at the end of its sentence, lends it a great deal of impact. It sets up the expectation that 'attention' will be developed – which, as we have seen already, is true.

Question

B *Lines 1–6*

Comment on the effect of each of the lists or series in this paragraph.

Answers on page 62

Expansion, explanation

Look at lines 21–24.

> Changing Rooms, Tool Stories, Home Front, you know the drill: take three couples, shuffle them with an interior designer/DIY expert/measly budget, see what sticks.

Here we have a colon performing one of its common functions – it introduces an explanation. But we have to be more specific in our comment. In this context, after the statement 'you know the drill' you are waiting for an explanation, because you don't, at this stage, know what the 'drill' is. The colon prepares you for the explanation which follows – the series of instructions/commands 'take three couples...' which is like a recipe. The ingredients in this case are contained in the phrase 'an interior designer/DIY expert/measly budget' structured in a shorthand way to suggest rapidly cheapening alternatives. It looks like a cynical formula unlikely to lead to success. The final command, 'see what sticks', is scathing about the result of the 'drill'. On the whole, the sentence structure here has the effect of being very critical of the programmes mentioned at the beginning of the sentence.

The use of 'And' at the beginning of a sentence.

The sentence which follows (lines 24–25) 'And if you thought we had reached saturation point, be warned, more are on the way' offers yet one more opportunity to comment on structure. 'And' at the beginning of a sentence is always used deliberately to isolate and to give extra prominence to an additional point the writer wants to make. It ought grammatically to be part of the previous sentence. The point here is about *yet another* DIY programme and it gains impact because the reader puts emphasis on *And* at the beginning of the sentence. The impression is that the previous programmes were bad enough but here comes another, possibly worse, example. It is not enough simply to say that 'And' gives prominence. There has to be an identification of what is made prominent and for what purpose.

Word choice

There are numerous examples of effective word choice in this article. It could be used in conjunction with the exercises in the section on Word Choice to provide further work in this area.

List of terms used:

- **sentence structure**
- **list**
- **series**
- **parallelism**
- **climax/anti-climax**
- **repetition**
- **expansion**
- **explanation**
- **colon/semi-colon**

- **short sentence**
- **minor sentence**
- **balance**
- **antithesis**
- **parenthesis**
- **point of view**
- **triad**
- **'And...' – position**
- **direct address**

nce Structure – further
ice

One of the techniques which the author of the following extract uses to influence and persuade you is careful sentence construction. You will notice that he uses a number of questions. The overall effect of this will depend on whether you feel that the questions require answers and that you, the reader, should be thinking about the problem; or whether you get fed up being beaten about the head by the sheer number of times you are asked to become involved. Apart from the questions, there are several other techniques which you can appreciate and analyse. To what extent they are effective is your decision.

Exercise

In the following extract from an article in the Sunday Herald *Ian Bell is mounting an attack on the sale of junk food to children.*

1   In a world that starves children to death routinely, losing your sense of humour isn't hard. If you also happen to sell opinions for a living, petty arguments can become big arguments with a few keystrokes. Suddenly every issue is a cataclysm, era-defining, and to order. That's expected.

5   Iraq? The matter is profound. Law and order? Someone will have lots to say. Nuclear power, global warming, genocide, refugees, economic apartheid, terrorism, truth, justice? Volumes are being written as you read this. I may have contributed.

Sometimes, for all that, it is worth remembering just how much the
10   mundane also matters. Little things. Small people. Everyday conundrums, domestic squabbles, those Monday morning compromises: what counts in the end is the world we inhabit. It probably counts for more, I suspect, than big, earnest newspaper columns.

So should you give a five-year-old a bag of crisps? If not, why not?
15   Try the questions in a different order. Why would a treat for an infant be problematic? Why on earth would an infant's treat be objectionable? If the 'treat' happens to be noxious, why would otherwise responsible, educated adults be trying very hard – and spending lots of someone's advertising money – just to persuade you to force a few ounces of processed potato
20   into a child's face against all medical advice?

➤

> The Food Standards Agency took a tiny little pop last week at Ofcom, the quango employed to regulate British broadcasting. The latter was attempting to come up with rules that might govern the advertising of junk food on TV; the former said the proposals were inadequate. Ban all junk ads before the
> 25 9p.m. watershed, said the FSA.
>
> Are these food 'stuffs' so potent a risk to the health of children that they need to be treated as drugs, treated, indeed, with the same caution we afford to alcohol and tobacco? Apparently so. The debate, remember, is over the risk of infants – all in bed before 8.59p.m., naturally – even hearing of salty,
> 30 sugary, saturated and wonderfully addictive treats.
>
> When you allow yourself to be defined as a consumer – and when you volunteer your children for training in that slavery – there is no end to the garbage you end up eating. Why are so many Americans so very large and so very miserable with their family-size jumbo kiddie meals? Because they have
> 35 been rendered into drugged units of bovine consumption. And why should we spare our children such a fate? Because healthy children are a delight. Because real life is beautiful.
>
> In the face of such a threat, we must ask ourselves why these tasty snacks are even legal and why we are still debating an 'appropriate' hour for
> 40 a cute cartoon.

Points to consider

In the following exercise you should be on the lookout for the effect of any or all of the techniques which were covered initially in the Exercise on page 13 such as: repetition, climax, anti-climax, minor sentences, lists or series, use of punctuation...

Remember that a list of techniques like this is an open list: you may use any of the above but there might also be other techniques which you could consider.

Questions

A (a) *Lines 5–8*
Identify two aspects of sentence structure and show how they effectively carry on the ideas of the first paragraph, especially 'Suddenly every issue is a cataclysm, era-defining, and to order.'

(b) *Lines 9–13*
Comment on the function of the colon in strengthening this part of his argument.

(c) *Line 14*
Show how this single line paragraph links paragraph 3 to paragraph 5.

(d) *Lines 15–20*
How does the punctuation in this paragraph contribute to the tone? You should consider two aspects of punctuation (apart from the question marks).

(e) *Lines 21–25*
How does the sentence structure help to mirror the opposition between the two organisations mentioned (Ofcom and the FSA)?

(f) *Lines 26–30*
Choose one aspect of sentence structure or punctuation in these lines which you consider to be effective in persuading or convincing you of the danger of advertising junk foods to children. Show how your chosen aspect achieves its effect.

(g) *Lines 31–37*
Show how repetition is used throughout this paragraph to strengthen the impact of his argument.

Answers on page 63

Concept Three

Information and Evidence

Among the Understanding questions generated by passages at Higher level there are some which ask you to isolate a number of points, or a number of pieces of evidence or a number of facts. The purpose of these questions is usually to see that you have been able to isolate ideas and understand them and their place within the passage. It helps to clarify your thoughts and allows you to see where a passage is going. An aid to finding your way through a passage like this and being able to isolate the main points and their relationships is to look at the words which act as **signposts**. Typical words of this kind are 'firstly', 'finally', 'now', and 'thus'.

There are similarities between this exercise and the one on Structure of an Argument (Concept Four). The skill of getting an **overview** of the passage by looking at the introduction, the topic sentences, and the ending is worth practising. It provides a way into an article.

Exercise

If we apply this process to the article from *New Scientist* below, the following points emerge:

- London is in danger of sinking – introduction in italics and headline
- Britain is sinking in the south – first **topic sentence**
- London is on the wrong site – last paragraph.

With this overview you are prepared to undertake an informed reading of the article. You know what it's about, and you know where it's leading.

Hillary Shaw writes about the difficulties likely to be encountered in the future in London.

Sinking London

1   Recent research shows that an adjustment in the weight applied to Britain's land surface is causing Britain to sink in the south and rise in the north. It is the result of a process called isostatic rebound. Since the last ice age, a huge burden of ice has been removed from the north of Britain. Because the Earth's crust is not rigid,
5   as it appears to us over a human life time, but very slightly elastic, it gradually responds to the addition or removal of weight above it by sinking or rising.

     This adjustment takes thousands of years. If you remove, say, a layer of rock 300 metres thick from the crust, this will rise some 200 metres, just as removing the cargo from a boat will make it rise higher in the water. Ice is
10   about a third the density of crustal rock, so removing 300 metres of ice will cause the crust to rise around 60 metres or so.

➤

Scandinavia and Scotland were under more than 300 metres of ice during the ice ages, and uplift is fastest in the northern Baltic, where it still continues at nearly a metre a century. This is easily noticeable even over a
15 human lifespan. The Hudson Bay area of Canada experiences a similar rate of uplift, for the same reason. In Britain the process is fastest in northeastern Scotland, where raised beaches exist several metres above the present sea level.

So why is the south of England sinking?
20 First, the burden of Scottish ice pushed up the crust in surrounding areas that were ice-free, just as pressing down on one part of a water bed makes adjacent areas of it rise. That process is now in reverse: the once-raised regions of Southern England and the southern Baltic are now sinking.

Secondly, sea level is rising worldwide. Once it rose rapidly as the ice
25 sheets over places like Scotland melted. Now global warming may be melting glaciers, sending more melt-water into the oceans. As the oceans grow warmer, thermal expansion also raises sea level.

Thus the south of England gets a double whammy – sinking crust and rising sea level. And the London area is subjected to a quintuple whammy.
30 Apart from the two factors already mentioned, the Thames Valley is a syncline, an area of locally subsided crust. Also, until recently groundwater extracted from below London was causing further subsidence. Finally, the funnel shape of the North Sea tends to bank up storm surges to ever greater heights as they enter the Thames Estuary.
35 All this adds up to one inescapable fact: the lower Thames was not a good place to site a major capital city.

Points to consider

Structure

If you were asked to say how this passage was structured you would look closely at the topic sentence whose main point is: Britain is sinking in the south and rising in the north.

The first three paragraphs deal with this geological process of land rising over time:

- Britain is sinking in the south and rising in the north.
- This rising takes thousands of years.
- The process is still going on.

There follows the key question 'So why is the south of England sinking?'

The signposts in the second half are very clear and simple:

- First,
- Secondly,
- Thus (the south of England gets a double whammy)
- All this adds up to...

Content

With an idea of the general structure in our minds we are now ready to tackle the detail of the content.

In this kind of informative writing there are likely to be **definitions**, **illustrations** and **expansions** of points – all designed to help your understanding of the concepts and processes involved.

Question

A Look at the second half of the article from line 19 onwards.

Identify all the words or phrases which you think are signposts.

Identify an example of an illustration which clarifies the meaning.

Identify two developments which expand on an initial short statement of fact.

Identify a scientific term and its attendant definition.

Answers on page 66

Typical questions on such articles will ask you to show your understanding of these features and to explain what is happening or being described. They would ask you to pick out and explain the various main points made.

They would also expect you to put the answer in your own words. Even if the question doesn't specifically ask you to do this, there is a general instruction on the front of the Question paper:

> **Use your own words whenever possible and particularly when you are instructed to do so.**

You have to be sensible about how far it is possible to use your own words. In the exercise which you are about to do about isolating 'the main points', there is no point in changing 'sink in the south and rise in the north'. What you should be looking to recast in your own words are phrases like 'the Earth's crust is not rigid' if these are among the main points required in the answer.

Questions

B (a) An explanation of 'isostatic rebound' is given in lines 3–6. In your own words attempt to give a definition.

(b) What is the meaning of the word 'elastic' in the context of lines 4–6? How does the context help you to arrive at the meaning?

(c) Show how the illustration about the boat (lines 8–9) helps you to understand the process.

(d) As briefly as possible say what two aspects of the process are dealt with in paragraph two (lines 7–11).

(e) In paragraph three (lines 12–18) what proof is given for the process of uplift?

(f) Show how effective the sentence 'So why is the south of England sinking?' (line 19) is in the structure of the passage.

(g) Summarise the two main reasons given in answer to the question posed in line 19?

(h) Using your own words as far as possible, list the factors which contribute to the 'quintuple whammy' to which London is subjected (lines 28–34).

(i) How effective is the last paragraph (lines 35–36) as a conclusion to the passage as a whole?

Answers on page 66

List of terms used:

- **topic sentence**
- **structure**
- **signposts**
- **definition**
- **illustration**
- **expansion**

- **overview**
- **summarise**
- **conclusion**
- **linking**
- **context and meaning**

Information and Evidence – further practice

This exercise allows further practice in dealing with Understanding questions. In it you will be asked to isolate a number of points, or a number of pieces of evidence or a number of facts. The purpose of questions such as these is usually to help to clarify your thoughts and allow you to see where a passage is going.

Exercise

In this case you can immediately get an overview of the passage by looking at the introduction in italics and the last sentence.

Look at the following extract from Clean and Decent – the fascinating history of the bathroom and the WC *written in 1960 by Lawrence Wright.*

> 1   In prehistoric times, early man held the belief that the beneficent provisions of nature have a divine origin. He felt that elements such as water represented powers greater than himself. Priests who developed this idea were wise enough to understand something of the effects of pollution, and
> 5   to make magic or religion the basis for sanitary taboos. They would not waste breath explaining these effects. It was simpler to make the water supply sacred, and to give warning that any interference with it could arouse divine wrath. Hence the reverence for sources, springs and pools where sacred bathing rites took place.
> 10   The purpose-built bath has had very different meanings, purposes and methods at different times in history. In Greece it was an adjunct to gymnastics: brief, cold and invigorating. In Rome it meant relaxation, bodily refreshment and resultant well-being; the basic method was to use steam and water in a succession of varying temperatures. It was a social duty, carried out in
> 15   company. The Greek or Roman bath was only incidentally a cleaning process. *Sanitas* (giving us our word 'sanitary') meant health, not the removal of dirt.
> In the Middle Ages, the communal bath, and the Turkish bath in its many imitations in Europe, had a similar leisure and social purpose. In the mediaeval monastery, however, the bath was strictly a routine cleaning, not
> 20   to linger over, not to be enjoyed, and perhaps to be imposed - icy cold - as a penance. At times the bath has been used as a symbolic rite, its pleasures and its cleansing being both purely spiritual. In the eighteenth and
>
> ➤

nineteenth centuries in Europe the bath normally implied medical treatment: the bather was 'the patient'.

25 From about 1860 the bath revived as a private routine cleaning, but with something of the monastic penance in the preference for cold water. With the coming of liberal hot water, it became once more permissible to enjoy one's bath, and to its purpose of routine cleaning is added today a dash of Roman relaxation.

Points to consider

Structure

The first paragraph is a philosophical introduction to the development of bathing rites. Thereafter the structure is very clear: the topic sentence (lines 10–11) 'The purpose-built bath has had very different meanings, purposes and methods at different times in history' announces three aspects of the purpose-built bath which the author will develop: meanings, purposes and methods within a historical framework.

Question

A By quoting words which act as signposts or links, show how the structure of the passage is based on the idea of 'at different times in history'.

Answer on page 71

Content

In each of the paragraphs from 'The purpose built bath...' (line 10) there are several main points made about the importance and purpose of bathing at different times and periods.

Typical questions about such a passage might ask you to pick up on the development of the topic sentence, or ask for evidence or isolate a number of points. Remember that in these Understanding questions especially you must use your own words (even when you are not specifically told to) to show that you have grasped the meaning of the details of the content.

Questions

B (a) Show how 'meaning, purpose and development' is exemplified with respect to the Roman bath (lines 12–15).

(b) Using your own words as far as possible write down:

Three main points from paragraph 2 (lines 10–16)

Four main points from paragraph 3 (lines 17–24)

Two main points from paragraph 4 (lines 25–29).

Answers on page 71

Deducing meaning from context

So far we have not looked closely at paragraph 1 (lines 1–9). There is really only one main point in the paragraph. The topic sentence of the paragraph is: 'In prehistoric times, early man held the belief that the beneficent provisions of nature have a divine origin.' This is quite a mouthful, and not immediately understandable. But help is at hand. The second sentence, 'He felt that elements such as water represented powers greater than himself' is, in fact, 'translating' the first sentence for us.

Early man held the belief	the beneficent provisions of nature	have a divine origin
↓	↓	↓
He (early man) felt	elements such as water	powers greater than himself

In other words, that water was such a benefit it had to be God-given and therefore sacred. The remainder of the paragraph down to line 9 is a development of this idea. See if you can follow this development by answering the following questions. (Remember to answer in your own words.)

Questions

C (a) Explain what the priests did to stop people polluting the water and what effect this had.

(b) What phrase in the first paragraph prepares for the concept of the 'purpose-built bath'?

Answers on page 71

Structure of an Argument

This exercise is closely linked to the exercise on Sentence Structure (page 13).

Following the structure of an argument is a skill which needs to be developed in order to take in the main points of the writer's views on the topic she is writing about. An argument has nothing to do with a quarrel. In its academic sense, as it is used here, it is concerned with the structure or framework within which a topic is discussed.

One of the basic structures is: introduction, one aspect of the topic, followed by a 'but' with another aspect of the topic, leading to a conclusion. You may have used this structure yourself in writing a discursive essay.

Most professional writers and journalists, however, use more complex structures because they have to make sure that they do several other things: they must attract the reader's attention; they must put points in a persuasive order; they must provide clarifying illustration or anecdote; they may feel the necessity to entertain; and they wish to bring the reader into agreement with their point of view by the end of the chapter or article.

In order to do this they use many devices. Among these they use words which act as signposts/links. (The simplest are those that join or contrast sections of evidence or argument – such as 'and', 'or', 'but', 'also', 'however'; whereas others might point to a conclusion: 'so', 'therefore'.) They use linking sentences. They use the structure of the sentences themselves to create questions, expectations, explanations, expansions, and turning points, and use them in combinations (such as repetition, balance, parallels) to sharpen the argument. There are also some small common words which can subtly influence the course or intensity of the argument. Words such as 'just', 'even', 'surely' or 'clearly' often intensify (or dilute) a statement. For example, 'Even the manager agreed with the decision' is obviously a stronger endorsement for the decision than 'The manager agreed with the decision.'

Exercise

In order to see these ideas in action read the following article by Ian Bell which appeared in the *Sunday Herald* in February 2006.

As always it is helpful to get an overview of an article before approaching the detail of the tasks.

- Introduction – elephants taking revenge/after victimisation
- Title – how to break the cycle of revenge?
- Last sentences – bleak conclusion (we) 'claim the same excuse' (as elephants)

There are magazine reports that something peculiar seems to be going on: the elephants appear to be taking revenge on human beings for past cruelties, in Africa and in India.

> **An eye for an eye, a tusk for a tusk … how do we break the cycle of revenge?**
>
> 1   Do elephants truly possess the capacity for such an emotion? Researchers believe so. If they are right, we need to think again about the relationship between humans and some animals. It is one thing to believe that we have a moral duty to avoid cruelty towards noble beasts. It is another thing from a
>
> 5   practical point of view if an elephant is charging at you and saying, in effect: 'You killed my mother. Now it's your turn.'
>
> This, at least, is the rough outline of the explanation offered by scientists. They believe that poaching, during the 1980s and before, left generations of young elephants, young males in particular, parentless, leaderless,
>
> 10   traumatised and unusually aggressive. In Uganda, today, they face no population pressures, nor is there any shortage of food. Instead, they seem to be attacking villages and blocking roads just because they feel like it.
>
> Or rather, because they do not like humans. As one researcher reports from India, elephants left to their own devices in remote areas tend to be
>
> 15   placid and tolerant. On the other hand, 'the more human beings they see, the less tolerant they become'.
>
> Given mankind's record in dealing with other species, you can't blame the elephants for that. They are not stupid creatures and their memories are indeed good enough to allow them to remember acts of cruelty and
>
> 20   violence: in other words, they have motive. Add opportunity and you have what homo sapiens would call revenge.
>
> If that is so, the questions come thick and fast. Creatures capable of bearing a grudge surely possess the elements of what we, of all animals, would recognise as a society. Haven't we spent millennia regarding
>
> 25   ourselves as the only beasts capable of understanding the idea of revenge? So what do we actually understand by the word? With all due respect to the raging bull elephants, it must involve some fairly primitive emotion: the elephants are not writing letters to the press demanding an apology from the Ugandan people, after all; they are, in fact, attacking humans aggressively.
>
> 30   If these reports are reliable, we have a lesson on our hands. Even among the elephants, the desire for revenge is born of pain, trauma, and cruelty. And is that not even more so in our own species which seems wedded to revenge?
>
> Such revenge may represent a primitive emotion, but that emotion has enduring, destructive power. The disease is an ancient, global pandemic. Like
>
> 35   Uganda's elephants we could all probably stand a psycho-therapeutic course in anger management. The common feature, the unlikely connection, is that the destructive pachyderms first had to be victimised before they could feel a need for victims. There is not a human society on the planet that does not claim the same excuse.

Points to consider

The argument may seem quite complex on first reading. It helps, usually, to look at the first paragraph in order to find what the topic of the article is going to be. You already have the little introduction in italics to help you, and also the title. In this article, if you don't look at those then the first sentence is not going to mean very much to you. What is 'such an emotion'? Obviously 'such' refers back to something which has already been mentioned; in this case, 'revenge'. The first sentence is framed as a question, so you would expect some proof (or otherwise) of this statement. The next step is to look at the conclusion to the article. '**Like Uganda's elephants. . .The common feature. . .There is not a human society on the planet that does not claim the same excuse.**' What seems likely is that somewhere in the article a parallel is going to be drawn between the behaviour of elephants and the behaviour of humans. You don't need to go any further than that at the moment because you hope now that any detailed work you do on the 'argument' will help you to a clearer understanding of the article.

Let's take the first two paragraphs. If we underline the words which help us towards the connections and links we get something like this.

> Do elephants truly possess the capacity for such an emotion? (Question)
> Researchers believe so. (Answer) If they are right, we need to think again about
> the relationship between humans and some animals. It is one thing to believe
> that we have a moral duty to avoid cruelty towards noble beasts. It is another
> thing from a practical point of view if an elephant is charging at you and saying,
> in effect: 'You killed my mother. Now it's your turn.'

> This, (link back) at least, is the rough outline of the explanation offered by
> scientists. They believe that poaching, during the 1980s and before, left generations
> of young elephants, young males in particular, parentless, leaderless, traumatised
> and unusually aggressive. In Uganda, today, (time link) they face no population
> pressures, nor is there any shortage of food. (structural repetition) Instead, they
> seem to be attacking villages and blocking roads just because they feel like it.

The opening sentence poses a question which we hope the article will answer. The reply 'Researchers believe so' leads us to expect that the research will be laid out and will convince us that elephants do, indeed, feel the need for revenge.

'If they are right' suggests that there will be consequences for humans and that these consequences will be to do with the 'relationship' between men and elephants.

The twin phrases, 'It is one thing' and 'It is another thing' alert us to a contrast. So we should look for the contrast in order to help us with this bit of the argument. The two words which contrast are 'moral' and 'practical'. And these highlight the 'moral' aspect of our relationship with elephants – we *should* be kind to them – with the 'practical' aspect that we *have to be* kind to them because they might take revenge on us if we are not.

Moving on to the next paragraph: 'This, at least, is the rough outline of the explanation offered by scientists.' Here we have a linking sentence. 'This . . . rough outline' refers back to the human idea of revenge encapsulated in 'You killed my mother. Now it's your turn' and 'the explanation offered by the scientists' which is more succinctly (four adjectives) and scientifically expressed in the rest of the paragraph which follows – the explanation that poaching was the cause of their otherwise inexplicable aggression.

Analysing the link in this amount of detail makes absolutely sure that you know where the argument is heading.

Questions

A *Paragraph 3 (lines 13–16)*
   (a) Continue identifying any of the sentences, words or phrases which seem to you to be important to the argument – links, repetitions, intensifying words, turning points, contrasts, parallels…

   (b) How does the first sentence in the paragraph act as a link?

   (c) Briefly, what is the contrast between the two behaviours attributed to elephants? How do the signposts help to structure the idea clearly?

B *Paragraph 4 (lines 17–21)*
   (a) Continue identifying any of the sentences, words or phrases which seem to you to be important to the argument – links, repetitions, intensifying words, turning points, contrasts, parallels…

   (b) How does the first sentence in this paragraph act as a link?

   (c) In what way is the phrase 'In other words' useful for clarifying the argument in this paragraph?

C *Paragraph 5 (lines 22–32)*
   (a) Continue identifying any of the sentences, words or phrases which seem to you to be important to the argument – links, repetitions, intensifying words, turning points, contrasts, parallels…

   (b) How does the first sentence in this paragraph act as a link?

   (c) Show how the punctuation of the sentence beginning 'With all due respect…' (line 26) helps to clarify the argument.

   (d) How does repetition help to mark the shift to the importance of the 'lesson' that 'we' have to learn?

   (e) Explain how intensifiers in lines 30–32 help to strengthen the argument.

D *Paragraph 6 (lines 33–39)*
   (a) Continue identifying any of the sentences, words or phrases which seem to you to be important to the argument – links, repetitions, intensifying words, turning points, contrasts, parallels…

   (b) How do the last three sentences from 'Like Uganda's elephants…' (lines 34–3 make an effective final connection between elephants and humans?

Answers on page 72

List of terms used:

- **argument**
- **introduction**
- **development**
- **conclusion**
- **illustrative anecdote**
- **point of view**
- **signposts**
- **links**
- **questions**
- **expectations**
- **premise**

- **explanations**
- **expansions**
- **turning point**
- **repetition**
- **balance**
- **parallel structure**
- **contrast**
- **consequences**
- **intensifiers**
- **imagery**

As you will have observed in examining this passage, an argument is developed through frequent and close linking, reinforced by parallel and balancing sentence structures and illustration/expansion. A further important sentence structure in argument is the 'if… then…' construction, often known as **premise** (if…) and **consequence** (then…): if you accept the first half, you are then supposedly bound to accept the second.

Structure of Argument can also be analysed in other passages in this Part of the book: on surveillance (page 4), junk food (page 18) and the Olympics (page 46), for example.

Remember also to consider the writer's point of view or stance. Some of these articles give very little credit to any other point of view, and choose their evidence very selectively.

Structure of an Argument – further practice

Exercise

For the article which follows you should first of all get an overview by looking at:

- Introduction (in italics)
- Headline
- First sentence
- Last sentence

All of these deal with two aspects of education: the building and what goes on inside it. The last sentence contains two contrasts: village/factory and Southwark/Ladakh.

Jonathan Glancey asks the question about what sort of buildings we want children to learn in, and what sort of education we want them to have in them.

A Classroom With a View

1   The most inspiring new school I know of, certainly from an architectural perspective, is the Druk White Lotus school, in Ladakh in India. Set high in the Himalayas, this beautiful, ecologically sound centre of excellence is like some very special village. Built mostly of timber and stone, and neither
5   overtly modern nor cloyingly traditional, it is a wonderfully refreshing design, a place where children long to be.

Clearly, with snow-capped Himalayan peaks to look at from their classroom windows, rather than housing estates, ring roads or traffic jams, the children attending the Druk White Lotus school are obviously at an
10   advantage, in terms of location and sheer aesthetics, over their peers battling their way through life in run-down parts of Britain. What teachers and architects might learn from the Ladakh experience, however, has more to do with the ways in which a school can be a genuine and welcoming meeting place - somewhere children and those charged with their education really
15   want to go to - than with its architecture as such.

If new schools are to be little more than machines for producing successful economic units in the guise of teenagers armed with exam certificates, then they will be failures as nurseries for a healthy society, even if their buildings are as beautiful as the Alhambra or the Taj Mahal. If, instead,
20   they aim at cultivating intelligent, imaginative, graceful souls with a hunger

➢

for knowledge and a love of learning, then they will have succeeded, even if their classrooms are little more than Nissen huts.

So school with a soul needs to be welcoming. One of the best reconstructions of what had been a failing inner-city school is that of the
25 Kingsdale school in Southwark. Its architect, Alex de Rijke discovered when he first visited the school how unwelcoming it was. With its long, dark corridors and horrible lavatories, it was a centre of bullying rather than education. What the school lacked was both light and a proper meeting place. De Rijke designed a handsome internal village centre, by covering
30 over an old external courtyard with a bright, lightweight roof that looks fun, and is cheap and practical. This created a place where children felt happy to meet, especially on damp, cold and generally miserable days.

The proper emphasis should be on creating sociable, enjoyable spaces, rather than machines for learning in. Architects from all over the world are
35 clearly able to design the former. But the big question hovering over the summit is, perhaps, do we really want schools to be like this in money-mad Britain? Surely the emphasis must be on hard, shiny academies turning out compliant, competent human cogs for further economic growth?

Perhaps, perhaps not. If a school was more like a village than a factory, a
40 place where people of different ages, backgrounds and abilities met happily rather than confronted one another, it would be somewhere special everyone might enjoy, whether in Southwark or Ladakh.

The questions which follow are mostly Understanding questions, and should all be answered as far as possible in your own words. This instruction need not be included in each question because you are expected to use your own words as far as possible throughout the Close Reading paper in the exam. Here it is just given as a reminder.

Before you embark on the following tasks, look for examples of the kinds of markers which belong to this sort of argumentative writing (see the exercise on page 28). You might like to think about links and signposts, structures for contrast and explanation, words like 'just', 'even', which influence the ideas . . .

Questions

A *Paragraph 1 (lines 1–6)*
How does the writer develop the idea of an 'inspiring' new school:

(a) from an architectural point of view?

(b) as a 'centre of excellence' for learning?

Paragraph 2 (lines 7–15)
(a) How is the ambience of Ladakh school contrasted with a British school?

(b) What implied criticism is made of a British school as an educational centre?

Paragraph 3 (lines 16–22)
(a) Write down the signposts which direct you towards the parallel structure.

(b) What two contrasting views of the purpose of education does the writer develop?

(c) How far is the architecture of the school building relevant to this?

Paragraph 4 (lines 23–32)
(a) Show how the first sentence performs a linking function.

(b) How does the author develop the main idea through his anecdote about architecture?

Paragraph 5 (lines 33–38)
(a) How does the topic sentence again contrast the two views of education?

(b) What is an obstacle to his preferred view of education in modern Britain?

(c) How is the image of 'machines' developed later in the paragraph and how does he hope this imagery will persuade you to his opinion?

Paragraph 6 (lines 39–42)
(a) How effective is 'Perhaps, perhaps not' as a link in the argument?

(b) By identifying specific words and phrases show how the final paragraph sums up ideas from the whole article.

Answers on page 75

Concept Five

Imagery

The discussion of imagery is the most interesting and most rewarding part of Close Reading. Close examination of imagery allows you to share the experience of the writer almost at first hand, making his thoughts your thoughts. A writer uses an image – a simile or a metaphor – because he has seen or felt or been searching for a comparison which allows him to pass on to you his feelings and emotions at the immediate moment of experience. Imagery is a kind of shorthand that allows an experience to be transferred from the imagination of the writer to the imagination of the reader without necessarily going through a logical process. That's why it is 'magic' – in all senses of the word.

Exercise

Look at the following extract from the book Summit Fever *by Andrew Greig. In it he is describing the approach marches to the high peaks of the Himalayas.*

> 1   The scale of it all and the sheer desolation were a shock to the mind and body. It scooped us out of ourselves like the stars do. It left us feeling tiny and liberated, finally jolted us free from the shell of our supposed importance.
>
> 5   Then we came on small villages, little miracles of fertility in the wilderness. I'd look up and see a straight green line slashed as if by a razor, slanting down across the cliffs, and know that it bled water and round the next bend would be human habitation, made possible by that lifeline of water channelled off a melting snowfield. The villages grew more grubby
>
> 10   and more lovely as we drove hour after hour deeper into the mountains. The path loped along by the irrigation channels. Some were clear, some muddy, some had no water in, only damp silt. I began to appreciate the extreme simplicity and complexity of the system that allowed the villagers to flood, moisten, and let dry out, according to daily need, what was
>
> 15   probably over a hundred fields spread out over an area of hillside roughly a mile and a half wide and the same in length. It was a network as complex and organic as the circulation of the blood, divided similarly into main arteries, veins, capillaries. I saw the sun flash on the spade of a villager half a mile up the hill; three minutes later the channel at my feet filled with
>
> 20   muddy, silt-laden water. I stood and watched the life force of the village snake its way downhill, branching out, flooding out across some fields and passing others by. An aged man below who appeared to be passing by

chance bent down and removed a small stone from the junction of two
channels, and the water took off on an entirely new tack across the fields.

25   It was as subtle and simple as water itself.

The next morning was pure joy. I set off early on the rising track that
snaked across the hillside. It was clear and cold, the rising sun levelled mile-
long shadows across the valley, the great peaks stood frozen to attention
against the high-altitude dark-blue sky. I was out in front, the only living

30   being in sight. I was an arrow, moving further and further away from the
tension that set me going, getting nearer and nearer my destination. After the
uncertainties and setbacks of the last weeks, nothing could stop me getting
there now.

Points to Consider

In this descriptive passage Greig is obviously using all the literary weapons that he
has available. He uses carefully chosen words and many similes and metaphors. He
has obviously found the Himalayan landscape both beautiful and fascinating and he
wants to convey to us the force with which all these impressions hit him, so that we
can share his excitement and wonder.

In the first paragraph the writer is trying to convey how vast the emptiness of the
mountains was and how small it made him feel. He uses simile and metaphor to try
to convey that feeling to us.

> The scale of it all and the sheer desolation . . . scooped us out of ourselves like
> the stars do.

> . . . finally jolted us free from the shell of our supposed importance.

He is saying that the scale and emptiness of the landscape is as vast and as empty as
the stars and the space surrounding them, and has the same effect on him. So you are
getting an impression of the cold and of the infinity of space surrounding and
possibly overwhelming him.

But what is he getting at when he says 'scooped us out of ourselves'? Does it suggest
'left us feeling hollow' as if our souls had been sucked out by the vastness of the
space? Or took our needs and desires away to leave only a love of the universe?
These are possible ideas based on the literal meaning of 'scooped' – hollowed out.
Perhaps further clarification arrives with the metaphor of the 'shell'. 'Free from the
shell of our supposed importance' suggests that our self-centredness interferes
with our appreciation of the really important transcendent and infinite beauty or
power or unknowableness of the universe, and that at moments which
he is describing the self can become unimportant, freed from its own
limitations.

Remember that the basis for a metaphor is a statement which is not 'true'. Human beings do not have 'shells' in the literal sense. The combination of 'scoop' and 'shell' suggests literally that we can be freed from our limitations in the same way as a sea creature can be flipped out of its shell, or perhaps even in the way a bird can be liberated from the prison of its shell.

There are other possible interpretations which will depend on the reader's receptivity to the imagery the writer has used. Any appropriate interpretation involving the literal meaning of the 'image' words (the 'root', if you like) and their extension into the figurative or metaphorical ideas which they spark off – space, cold, emptiness, freedom, infinity…will be acceptable.

The process usually involves:

- Identifying the actual words of the image
- Specifying the initial literal/denotative meaning – the root
- Applying the shared aspects of the connotational area of the root
- Showing how all of these have combined to create a striking comparison which is effective in relaying the writer's experience, emotions and perceptions.

In the next paragraph we can identify imagery in a number of words or phrases.

> Then we came on small villages, <u>little miracles of fertility</u> in the wilderness. I'd look up and see <u>a straight green line slashed as if by a razor</u>, slanting down across the cliffs, and know that <u>it bled water</u> and round the next bend would be human habitation, made possible by that <u>lifeline of water</u> channelled off a melting snowfield. The villages grew more grubby and more lovely as we drove hour after hour deeper into the mountains.

An adequate commentary on 'little miracles of fertility' would suggest that the small villages which he came across should, in the middle of the general wild and inhospitable conditions, be barren, but the fact that they were productive, green, seemed inexplicable and marvellous, as were the original biblical miracles. This image contributes to the overall sense of wonder which the writer feels.

The unexpected pairing 'bled/water' juxtaposes the blunt monosyllable 'bled', with its suggestion of life blood oozing from a wound, against the unexpected word 'water', with its associations with life-giving liquid. This contrast conveys the wonder and shock of vegetation appearing in a desert, reinforcing the idea of 'miracle'.

Questions

A What impressions do the images 'a straight green line slashed as if by a razor' and 'lifeline of water' convey?

B Take each of the following images and show how each conveys effectively the writer's feelings when faced with these experiences.

(a) 'loped along' (line 11)

(b) 'It was a network as complex and organic as the circulation of the blood, divided similarly into main arteries, veins, capillaries.' (lines 16–18).

(c) 'new tack' (line 24)

(d) 'the great peaks stood frozen to attention' (line 28)

(e) 'I was an arrow, moving further and further away from the tension that set me going, getting nearer and nearer my destination.' (lines 30–31)

Answers on page 77

List of terms used:

- **metaphor**
- **simile**
- **personification**
- **incongruity**
- **connotation**
- **hyperbole**

- **root and extension**
- **figurative**
- **identify**
- **specify**
- **apply**
- **tone**

Imagery – further practice

To make sure that you start this exercise on the right foot, look at the introduction to the article and think what tone is suggested by the phrase 'outbreak of sisterly love'.

Exercise

Sylvia Patterson writes in the Sunday Herald Magazine *about the outbreak of sisterly love at the Glamour Women Of The Year Awards.*

1   You may have wondered, momentarily, how it feels to walk down one of those red carpets and be confronted by 60 photographers training their lenses, as big and black as a hole in outer space, straight on to your every pore, fibre and follicle. It's mortifying; more mortifying than walking down
5   the high street naked because you're walking down the high street naked and scores of women who are paid several million pounds for being professionally beautiful have just walked naked down the high street before you.

    You walk this crimson plank looking anywhere but straight at the lenses,
10   which have lights on top as blinding as the Caribbean sun, which have glaringly checked you out, decided 'It's okay, it's nobody' and a part of you thinks 'come on chaps, you could've pressed a button . . . accidentally!?'

    Naomi Campbell then flounces down the carpet like a selection of knitting needles thrown up a close into a newborn nebula of flashbulbs
15   exploding in infinity. No wonder they're Them and you're you: Naomi Campbell and the womanly glitterati are not, as you are, disguising scuffs on your once-fabulous white shoes with copious amounts of Tippex. But if you were one of Them, the lensmen would've noticed, and exposed your 'Chav shoe horror!' to the globally snickering world. . .
20   The Glamour Women Of The Year Awards, 2006, this year, wasn't characterised by the bitching, back-stabbing and torch-tongued jealousy which usually defines celeb culture today but by a blanket outbreak of sisterly solidarity.

    Teri Hatcher took to the podium and ripped out her hair extensions, her
25   'extra confidence hair' which she would now live without, declaring women's lot today 'is always about struggling and being envious and trying to find worth and confidence in ourselves and there's the illusion that somehow all this is so fabulous and easy and . . . honest. It isn't! We're all the same underneath and at the end of the day we're just gonna be . . . dead!'
30   Scores of the world's most glamorous women riotously applauded.

Points to Consider

One would hope that the answer you arrived at was that the tone suggested by the introduction was ironic, amused, sarcastic.

This tone is contributed to by the contrast between 'sisterly love' which might already suggest irony, and the metaphor 'outbreak' and its association with the beginning of a war. The effect is humorous, suggesting that peace will not last or is only skin deep.

Questions

A (a) Identify one metaphor and one simile in lines 1–4.

(b) Choose one of these and comment on how it highlights the uneasiness the writer says she feels when walking down the red carpet.

(c) What metaphor is being used in the second paragraph to exacerbate the uneasiness created by the red carpet? How does this metaphor work and in what way does the simile which follows it add to the effectiveness?

(d) Look at the simile 'like a selection of knitting needles thrown up a close' (lines 13–14) used to describe the tall model, Naomi Campbell. What impression does the simile give of the model's appearance and movement? What does it suggest about the attitude of the writer?

(e) Look at the metaphor 'into a newborn nebula of flashbulbs exploding in infinity' (lines 14–15). What impression does this metaphor create about the atmosphere around the model? How is the writer using imagery to point up the contrast between her own and Naomi Campbell's reception?

(f) In lines 20–23 there are several words or phrases which have metaphorical connotations. For each word or phrase you identify show how the connotations contribute to a sarcastic, critical or bitchy tone.

(g) What effect does the last sentence have on your appreciation of the whole article?

Answers on page 80

Concept Six

Tone

Tone is a tricky concept to deal with in Close Reading. It is not a technique, as such. Tone is created by various techniques – structure, word choice, sound, point of view, juxtaposition, imagery, exaggeration, register, among others.

Note: You will find exercises on structure, word choice, imagery and exaggeration elsewhere in this book. Here is an explanation of the other techniques listed above.

Sound

The devices related to sound are rhyme, rhythm, repetition (of words or sounds or phrases), assonance and alliteration (which also depend on repetition of a particular kind). There are others, but these are the more common ones. As with all the other devices we have been discussing, merely to identify, for example, alliteration will not be enough. There has to be a comment on how the alliteration affects the impact, or the tone, or the mood of the communication.

Point of view (or writer's stance)

This is the angle from which a writer personally approaches the subject. The writer could be taking a position opposed to the cheap food policy of supermarkets, or, as in the article which follows, an anti-Winnie the Pooh stance.

Juxtaposition

This is simply putting two words or concepts deliberately next to each other which seem to be in some way opposed to each other, or incongruous. The effect of this can be to make you think again, or it can make you laugh.

Register

This means using language appropriate to the situation. For example, in a formal situation, in a job interview, or in a serious newspaper article, it would not be considered appropriate to use a lot of slang vocabulary and colloquial phrases. These aspects of language would be perfectly appropriate at a party with friends. The register chosen contributes to the tone of the communication.

It is also common to mix registers (formal/informal) for 'impact' because the English language has a stylistic weapon: words of similar denotation may have different connotations which derive from their origin in different languages – Greek/Latin/French, and Anglo-Saxon. These have contributed to the development of the English language. The Anglo-Saxon (common everyday English) words tend to be more homely, ordinary, down-to-earth, strongly emotional; whereas Greek/Latin and, to a great extent, French words are used in more formal intellectual contexts.

Consider, for example, the differences in connotation which you might find in the following:

- regal/royal/kingly
- contusion/bruise
- female/feminine/womanly
- epidemic/plague/disease/sickness
- petite/small
- grand/great

Now we return to the subject of the exercise – our discussion of tone.

The first necessity is to notice that a particular tone has been adopted. If the passages were read out to you in an appropriate tone, you would have no difficulty in recognising what was happening. That is because tone is created by 'voice'. You 'hear' the language as if someone were speaking it.

The words you use to identify tone are all words to do with speaking in a particular way. Words such as angry, wheedling, moaning, critical, humorous, doom-laden, hectoring, ironic all could describe a particular voice. (If you don't know what 'hectoring' means, look it up.)

If you are asked a question about tone, or tone is suggested as one of the aspects of language you might look at in a question, then you can be fairly sure that there will be an obvious and identifiable tone. But you have to do more than just identify it. You have to show what alerted you to the tone – which words or structures particularly suggested the tone you have identified. And you're still not finished: you have to relate the words you have chosen to the tone you have identified to show how they are linked.

Exercise

As it is always easier to work with real examples, let's look at the following short article by Morag O'Brien.

> ### Why I hate Winnie the Pooh
> 1 This mindless obsession for Winnie the Pooh spans generations. He's everybody's favourite bear. But why? What about Yogi and Boo Boo, and their comical quests for jelly sandwich-filled picnic baskets? Or the all-singing, all-dancing Jungle Book bear, Baloo? At least those beasts have a
> 5 personality – more than can be said for that scantily clad, fur-covered ball of lard.
> Let's face it, he's overweight and over-rated. How often has that thick, greedy bear underestimated the size of his backside and got stuck in a hole? Fat chance of creating a health-conscious society when children have the
> 10 likes of Winnie to look up to. When did you ever see him do a bit of exercise?
>
> ➤

> This ardent dislike springs from a chronic overload of Pooh-related merchandise throughout my childhood. That bear has got his grubby paws all over the mass market. Every way I turn I see his podgy profile, on
> 15 everything from earmuffs to egg cups.
>
> Pooh is not dissimilar to an aging rock star either. Will he ever take the hint that he's past his sell-by date? After all, it's 75 years this weekend since his birth in the first A.A. Milne book. Baloo, Yogi and Boo Boo have done the sensible thing and gracefully withdrawn from the limelight. So do us all a
> 20 favour, Pooh, and follow suit.

Points to consider

What is your overall impression of the tone of this article? Is it serious or humorous, critical or admiring, annoyed or accepting...?

It appears to be humorous, critical, slightly annoyed. It is not serious and angry. You could describe it as mocking, which contains elements of humour and criticism and irritation.

The title itself is an illustration of the tone. The strong word 'hate' is coupled with a harmless childhood character, so we are aware of some incongruity already, and incongruity, in the matter of tone, tends towards humour. (See the explanation on page 50.)

'This mindless obsession' uses strong word choice to create a critical tone. 'Obsession' and 'mindless' both suggest that the person concerned is irrational, but going on to talk about Winnie the Pooh and the other cartoon characters reduces the tone to mocking.

The structure of the sentence: 'At least those beasts have a personality – more than can be said for that scantily clad, fur-covered ball of lard,' uses the contrast of 'at least' with 'more than can be said' to point out the difference between the other bears and Pooh. The dash makes you wait for the critical statement – 'a scantily clad fur-covered ball of lard.' The impact of this statement depends on a number of things: sound, a monosyllabic description of Pooh, and a sense of climax.

The contribution of sound is illustrated by the concentration of 'c's and 'l's. The harsh 'c' suggests contempt, and the mouth filling 'l' sound in 'ball of lard' makes it sound disgusting. The word itself has connotations of greasiness. The fact that the final word of the sentence is a derogatory monosyllable creates a sense of satisfactory climax.

Both word choice and imagery contribute to the criticism of Pooh. The description, 'fur-covered ball of lard', is actually also a metaphor used to compare the shape and feel of 'a ball of lard' – round, squidgy, fat, but with a furred surface – with the shape of an overstuffed, pudgy toy bear. 'Scantily clad' is poking fun at Pooh's always-too-small jacket but there is also a comic sense of incongruity in that 'scantily clad' is more often used for sexy models. Both the word choice and the imagery support the critical but humorous tone.

In one paragraph we have been able to identify a tone, and justify our choice by reference to word choice, sentence structure, imagery, sound and the juxtaposition of incongruous concepts. Comments have been made to show how examples of these techniques have contributed to the tone.

Questions

A Look at the second paragraph, lines 7–11, and identify the contribution of sound, register, structure/punctuation towards the mocking tone.

B Look at the third paragraph (lines 12–15). By referring to the use of register, an example of imagery and an example of alliteration show how the mocking tone is maintained in this paragraph.

C How does the structure of the last sentence (lines 19–20) contribute to the feeling of finality and satisfaction in the conclusion of the article?

Answers on page 82

List of terms used:

- **sound (rhythm, assonance, alliteration)**
- **point of view**
- **incongruity**
- **monosyllabic**
- **structure**
- **positioning of words**
- **word choice**

- **juxtaposition**
- **register (formal/informal)**
- **connotation**
- **'voice'**
- **imagery**
- **exaggeration**

- **mood** (introduced on page 46–47)
- **atmosphere**
- **polemic**

Tone – further practice

In the following article there are, as usual, many techniques adopted by the writer to create a tone which will influence our thinking.

There are other aspects of writing which work rather in the same way as tone. Mood and atmosphere are also created by the use of a variety of literary techniques. As tone is identifiable as the 'voice' in which the article is 'said', so atmosphere is identifiable through the senses, as a sort of physical thing – sight, sound, smell... Mood is identifiable as something appreciated through the emotions – joy, sorrow, despair...

There is overlap among these three aspects of writing, and they often reinforce each other. An unpleasant atmosphere, or a depressed mood can contribute to an angry tone, for example.

The previous exercise on tone – Winnie the Pooh – was basically a light-hearted piece, entertaining in itself, having a swipe at children's merchandising. This article is different. The tone is not light-hearted.

Start by reading the introduction and the headline.

Then the first paragraph.

Then the last paragraph.

Exercise

Will Self last month visited the site of the Olympic Games in east London and, in this personal polemic, decides that the Olympics will 'represent a drain on our purses, a waste of our time and a new nadir in our national prestige'.

Not in my manor

1 However, it wasn't until we stood on the grey-green football pitches of Hackney Marsh and looked south to where the brutalist skyline of Canary Wharf thumped the low cloud cover that I realised we were looking at the future. For here, in among rusty oil bowsers and light industrial hugger-

5 mugger, is where Tony, Gordon, Tessa, Seb, Ken and all their yea-saying, log-rolling confrères are intent on building the New Jerusalem of the 2012 London Olympics.

  If the idea wasn't quite so preposterous, wasteful and deluded it would've made both of us roar with laughter, but as it was we meditated

10 grimly on the plan – already mooted – to tarmac over the pitch we stood on

➤

and turn it into a colossal car park for spectators. This sacrifice on the altar of 'sporting excellence' – a local sporting amenity bulldozed for spurious national pride – is just one of the thousands of dumb little undertakings that, taken together, will add up to a fiasco of truly Olympian proportions.

15 Take it from me, London – and Britain as a whole – will come out of 2012 with none of the following: a fitter and happier citizenry; better sports facilities; improved metropolitan transport infrastructure; a boosted economy.

On the contrary, the Olympics will represent a drain on our purses, a
20 waste of our time, a new nadir in our national prestige and a political debacle that will have public servants blaming each other, with the requisite and costly inquiries, for decades to come.

There's much talk among the sycophants who still remain loyal to the 'Blair project' of what the Great Leader's legacy will be. Some morons are
25 suggesting that 2012 will be the jewel in his crown.

But the idea that the 2012 Olympics will guarantee Blair's legacy is a delusion. In the past decade, central London has lost another 15 per cent of its Olympic-size public swimming pools; during the same period local authorities have continued to flog off their sports fields with gay abandon.
30 London is too big, too old and too anarchic to have its future determined by the Blair regime's Six-Year Plan. They may make compulsory purchases, tarmac over the sports pitches, roust out the travellers' encampments and tidy the urban detritus under their magic finance carpet, but very quickly it will all come tumbling back, the steely weeds of a city that has defied
35 everything that god, men or even planners can throw at it.

Having read the whole passage, you now know that Will Self is opposed to the Olympic Games being sited in this desolate part of London, and does not see that there will be any permanent benefit to the area arising out of the occasion.

Points to consider

The introduction to the passage described it as a '**polemic**'. This term is used to describe a very one-sided article. The writer's stance is obvious and his strongly-held views are communicated to you without any concessions to another point of view. On this occasion you were alerted to the extreme nature of the article in the introduction, but you should always be on your guard as a reader and be aware of how you are being manipulated.

Although the main point of this exercise is tone, there are questions which deal with the related concepts of mood and atmosphere.

Questions

A (a) What atmosphere is created in lines 1–7, and how does the word choice contribute to this?

(b) What seems to be the mood of the writer and his friend suggested in lines 8–11? Quote the word which conveys this mood.

(c) Read lines 11–18. Show how each of the following contributes to the bitter, derogatory tone that Will Self has adopted:

- imagery
- punctuation
- sentence structure

(d) How does the structure of the sentence beginning 'On the contrary' (line 19) affect the argument and the tone of the article?

(e) There is a change in register in lines 23–25. How does this affect the tone of the article?

(f) Quote words or phrases from the next paragraph (lines 26–29) which show another such change .

(g) How effective is the last sentence in bringing the argument of the article to its conclusion in terms of both ideas and style?

Answers on page 84

Concept Seven

Exaggeration

This feature of language, which is also known as hyperbole, is found in many kinds of writing. It can be used in satire with serious purpose, but its most common use is in achieving a comic effect. It is very closely associated with tone and can be used to create one which could be, for example, humorous or derisory or pejorative or indulgent or affectionate.

Exercise

Look at the following passage written by Jeremy Clarkson for his column in The Sunday Times.

The secret life of handbags

1   Recently I was told that the average man wastes 394 days sitting on the lavatory. That's 56 weeks, wailed the report despairingly. But 56 weeks is nothing compared with the amount of time I really do waste, standing outside the front door in the freezing cold waiting for my wife to find the

5   keys in her handbag.

And then there are the aeons I waste waiting for her to answer her mobile phone. Normally it rings for 48 hours before she finds it nestling at the bottom of her bag, underneath a receipt for something she bought in 1972. These days, if I suspect the phone is in her bag I write a letter instead.

10 It's quicker.

The American army think they have a tough time trying to find Osama Bin Laden, who is holed out in a cave somewhere in the mountains of Afghanistan. But really they should thank their lucky stars he didn't choose to hide out in my wife's handbag.

15 So what does she have in it then? Down below the crust, in the asthenosphere, we find a pair of spectacles that she doesn't need and three – that's not a misprint – three pairs of sunglasses. Which seems excessively optimistic, frankly. Why, I ask, do you have a pair of spectacles in your handbag when your eyes are fine? 'Well, I might need them at some point,' she said. So

20 does that mean there's a Stannah stairlift in there, and some incontinence pads?

Below the eyewear, in the upper mantle, there is some chewing gum, which she never eats, coins for countries that don't exist any more and pills for things that cleared up 15 years ago. I did not dare go further than this, into the inner core, for fear of finding the bones of Shergar. Or a secret

25 pocket being used by Lord Lucan.

➤

> I genuinely don't understand this need to carry everything you've ever owned around with you at all times. No, really, when you are out and about you don't need to have cough medicine for children who have already grown up and finished university. And if you don't believe me, ask a
> 30 man.

Points to consider

Obviously the passage is humorous in its description, from a man's (slightly misogynistic?) point of view, of the depths and the contents of a woman's handbag. But how is that humour created? We can all see that it is funny, but it is harder to analyse the language to show how the techniques which the writer uses are effective in making it so.

There are, of course, several techniques at work here which we will look at at the end of this exercise, but the one we will focus on initially is exaggeration.

A word which you may find useful in commenting on the humorous effects of language is '**incongruity**', or its adjective, '**incongruous**'. At its simplest, it means that things don't 'match'. In this case, the idea of any of the lifesize objects or people mentioned being inside the handbag is obviously a mismatch in scale, but the attempt to 'see' in your mind's eye, the tiny man inside the bag, leads to a comic effect. In cartoons you can see this effect in graphic form, but in words it is equally effective. It is a vital element in creating a sense of exaggeration.

Look at the second paragraph, lines 6–10.

Here are two very obvious and very straightforward examples of exaggeration:

- 'rings for 48 hours'
- 'receipt for something she bought in 1972'

Neither of these 'facts' can be true.

- 48 hours suggests that a long time, a time longer than could be thought humanly necessary, elapses before the phone is answered.
- 1972 suggests that the handbag has in it an accumulation of rubbish as if it has been hoarded for over 30 years.

In each case the exaggeration produces a derisory tone, mocking his wife's lack of organisation.

Questions

A (a) Show how references to time in the first paragraph (lines 1–5) set the exaggeration ball rolling.

(b) What is the source of the humour in the reference to 'a letter' in line 9?

(c) How does his reaction to his wife's comment 'Well, I might need them at some point' (line 19) intensify the preposterous tone of the article?

(d) How is the idea of stumbling across secreted objects made comic by the references to Shergar and Lord Lucan (lines 24–25).

Answers on page 88

All these examples of exaggeration so far have been based on single details or comparisons but there is a larger framing device helping to structure the whole article.

This is an extended image. The image starts with the use of 'crust' and 'asthenosphere' in lines 15–16.

Question

B Identify the words later on in the passage which continue this image and show how the image is effective in maintaining the humour.

Answer on page 89

Finally, there is a very individual tone to this article. The writer makes more than usual use of **intensifiers**: 'really do' (line 3); 'But really' (line 13) and 'No, really' (line 27).

> I <u>genuinely</u> don't understand this need to carry <u>everything</u> you've <u>ever</u> owned around with you at <u>all</u> times.' (lines 26-27)

Anyone who has heard Jeremy Clarkson speak will recognise his voice in this exaggerated delivery. There is also an obsessive insistence on the reality of the situation which is totally at variance with the fantasy he has created – another level of incongruity.

List of terms used:

- **incongruity**
- **extended image**
- **tone**
- **intensfiers**

- **hyperbole**
- **disproportional/dispartity**
- **framing device**

- **stance** (introduced on page 52)

Exaggeration – further practice

Exaggeration contributes towards tone. The earlier article on handbags was on the whole mildly critical, slightly mocking. In this next article the tone is more critical, sharper. The writer's **stance** is more obvious and the case she is attempting to make is ultimately more important than untidy handbags. The exaggeration expands, becoming wilder all the time, eventually creating a fantasy, an absurdly comic, cartoon world.

Fiona McCade writes about the proposition that school report cards should deal with health.

An obesity report card? Fat chance

1   Parents could soon be receiving report cards from schools, informing them that their kid is fat – if the SNP's latest bold initiative ever sees the light of day. They want to see annual health checks for children, with individual health plans that involve parents in making the necessary changes to diet
5   and exercise.

Apparently school nurses will have a big role to play in this, as soon as anyone can find one.

How could parents have failed to notice their children are fat? If they can't recognise that they have overlarded offspring, they must be even
10   fatter. And if mum and dad have no way of comparing themselves with normal-sized people, the almost inescapable conclusion is that there are whole cities in Scotland that contain only fat people and where you can waddle for days without seeing anybody weighing less than 20st. It could be true, I suppose, at a pinch.

15   It also makes you wonder what the report cards might say: 'Dear Mrs Scott, Hamish is now too wide to get through the school gates. If you care to operate the little crane that hoists you off the sofa and heaves you about the house, you might discover that he is at home for this very reason.

'PS. Hamish is the short, spherical warm thing standing by your open fridge.'

Questions

A   List examples of exaggeration from each of the following sections and write a brief comment on why you think the phrase you have identified is an exaggeration.

- Lines 6–7: one example
- Lines 8–14: three examples
- Lines 15–18: two examples
- Line 19: one example

B   Who do you think is the target of the ridicule in this short article?

Answers on page 90

Answers ✔

Word Choice

'Surveillance' – questions begin on page 6

A

Word	Denotation	Connotation and Effect
bottomless	very deep, limitless	also suggesting that we're not talking about the infinity of space, rather the 'bottomless pit' – often used as a reference to hell, suggesting disapproval
trawl	to catch fish with a trawl net pulling through the water	here it means to make lots of passes through the information to catch the slightest wrong-doing
stuff	worthless material/information	the suggestion is that a lot of this information is useless, trivial, unimportant, but it is still irresistibly tempting
warrantless	without justification or authorisation	this suggests the authorities are taking illegal liberties with our personal data
intrusion	sense of entering uninvited	here with the idea of thrusting in a forceful way like a burglar, intent on harm
dataminers	digging into data	mining has the connotations of networks of tunnels underground, working hard at getting at that which is hidden or difficult to retrieve but, in this context, attacking privacy
hard (intelligence)	definite, solid	there is a slight suggestion that the information is not to the benefit of the person, harsh, producing bad results
idle	lazy	the idea that even while doing almost nothing vast amounts of 'hard' information can be accumulated against a person

➢

Answers – Word Choice ✓

Word	Denotation	Connotation and Effect
tremble	shake	the connotations of this word with fear and alarm are possibly exaggerated but nevertheless show the writer's distaste for surveillance
massive	very large, weighty	this intensifies the scale of the government's extreme power by giving the impression of an extreme dimension

Commentary
The fact that the answers above appear in table form is only to help you identify the various strands. It is not necessarily the best way of answering this kind of question in the exam.

B (a) The inverted commas cause the reader to take a second look at what seems to be an important technical term and realise that it just means 'counting people's phone calls'.

(b) It means looking for frequency of phone calls concentrated in particular areas.

(c) 'Cluster patterns' is a description of a statistically significant group but also has connotations of concentration of incidences of disease (like CJD).

(d) A terrorist cell is a group of people whose purpose for meeting is to plan death and destruction; a bridge club is a group of people intent on pursuing a social, peaceful pastime.

(e) The inability on the part of NSA to distinguish between the two by merely counting phone calls seems to Raban a very fundamental flaw reflecting the stupidity or pointlessness of the activity as a security device. (See also the commentary on the answer to D – page 55).

Answers – Word Choice

C (a) 'Machinery': an engine that has been set into motion as an essential part of the NSA system. This suggests that there is an inevitability and unstoppability about the NSA systems as if they had been set in motion and no-one was likely to stop them;

'furniture (of life)' suggests that the apparatus of state security has become almost as familiar and unnoticed as the furniture people have around them in their homes – accepted rather than noticed.

(b) 'Magnetometer': sense of scientific expertise with perhaps a touch of absurdity/Starwars since it measures the earth's magnetic field(!).

'Bio Watch air sniffer': sense of absurdity/gobbledygook; the first two words might imply something cutting edge/pushing the boundaries but the other words' implications are so low tech that the whole term suggests something cobbled together, or something in the paranormal/psychic realm.

'Razor wire': suggests a very old-fashioned, barbaric, crude defence system.

(c) All three *together* send out totally different messages suggesting an undiscriminating willingness to try anything that might work (without real evaluation) or an organisation of crackpots with a variety of hare-brained ideas.

D '(Military) Reservation' – like territory set aside for Native Americans – suggests the poverty and isolation of the area is hardly suitable for such a national agency.

'Desolate acres' – empty miles of desert wasteland suggesting an isolation and lack of productivity.

'Ailing mushroom farm' – series of discoloured dilapidated domes seen from above suggests a process of decay and sickness.

All of these make the headquarters of this all-seeing agency with its obsession for secrecy seem rather pathetic and unimpressive, which adds to his critical view of surveillance and all its apparatus.

> *Commentary on D*
>
> In each case the denotation/connotation aspect of the word or phrase has been adequately dealt with, but the question 'What effect…on your impression of the importance of the NSA' is not answered until the sentence beginning 'All of these…'.
>
> This comment demonstrates that the link between connotation and effect has been made.

Answers – Word Choice

E

Word	Denotation	Connotation and Effect
immense	very large	connotations of extreme size – top of the scale, making the rocks seem more frightening
enormous	very large	connotations of extreme size – top of the scale, making the rocks seem more frightening
squared off	cut to look square	suggests the block-like nature of these rocks, their solidity and capacity to damage
lumps	big pieces	the connotations suggest features which are not attractive, shapeless masses looming over the scene threateningly
menace	danger	the connotations of 'menace' are more of the danger looming over, about to overwhelm; potential for danger at some unexpected moment

F

Word	Denotation	Connotation and Effect
softened, liquid-looking stones	rounded, washed with a film of water	this phrase suggests a kindly and benevolent set of rocks with little danger which contrast with the ones now visible
splinters	pieces of wood split off	here it suggests the destruction of the ship by turning the wood of which it was made into tiny pieces of debris
brassy light	yellow light	the connotations are metallic, harsh, and possibly dangerous
burned (beauty)	affected by heat	this suggests strong forces at work, other dangerous forces like fire

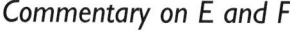

> **Commentary on E and F**
> Normally, when you are asked to deal with word choice it is only the connotations which will gain you credit. If you give simply the denotation, you are not dealing with the effectiveness of the word. However, it is good practice to start with the denotation so that you know that you must go beyond that. The fact that the answers above appear in table form is only to help you identify the various strands. It is not necessarily the best way of answering this kind of question in the exam.

G Imagery:

- 'a giant hell mouth ringed with black-tipped fangs'

  This suggests, literally, a large mouth with sharp teeth as in a mediaeval painting of the Last Judgement, but it gives the scary impression that the circle of rocks has a life of its own, and a hunger, with the desire to crush and devour any shipping.

- 'like (archetypal) sharks' fins'

  This simile compares the smaller rocks sticking out of the water with sharks' fins, which are the only part of the shark to stick out of the water, but which suggest the great danger that lies beneath.

- 'so sharp you could slice meat'

  This comparison suggests that the rocks are as sharp as an average butcher's knife and gives the impression that they could easily cut through something as solid as a boat.

- 'an Alcatraz'

  This is literally an island prison off San Francisco with the reputation of never letting any prisoners escape. Here the comparison is that any ship caught among these rocks would be completely unable to escape.

- 'rocks are the everlasting version of bullets and razor wire'

  Razor wire and bullets were literally those things which stopped prisoners escaping. In this comparison the rocks have the same deathly properties and so prevent any ship caught in their circle from getting free. Their dangers are as great as the bullets which kill escaping prisoners or the razor wire which cuts them to pieces should they reach the walls.

  Alcatraz and the bullets and razor wire could be dealt with together as an extended image.

Word Choice – further practice

'Mr Blobby' – questions begin on page 12

A For each of the following words, your answer should contain some idea of the connotational area the writer is exploiting, which touches on the deceptive nature of the activities. The most obvious connotations are given below.

Note: Remember that normally your answers would not be considered complete unless they contained comments on the deception involved as well.

Word	Denotation	Connotation
imaginative	created in the mind	made up, fanciful, far fetched, ineffective
expensive	highly priced	costing much more than they are worth, ridiculously dear
miraculous	beyond human power	suggesting supernatural results – beyond normal medical skill
claims	statements of efficacy	asserted in a boastful way without proof
quackery	the practice of fake doctors	ridiculous name making the idea of any scientific basis doubtful
parasitic	living on a host/another creature	growing rich by sucking sustenance out of others, giving nothing back
coined	newly invented	made up, for fraudulent purposes, to claim credibility
exploit	to take advantage of	make money out of a weaker person, manipulate weakness
innocents	naïve people	of childlike stupidity, willing to be led
fancy	elaborate	made to look imposing, complicated
flashy	superficial	fashionable, expensive looking
black box	packaging	suggests sophisticated, rich contents, magic properties

➤

Answers – Word Choice further practice

Word	Denotation	Connotation
fads	fashions of the moment	foolish, temporary enthusiasms
scams	fraudulent schemes	cheap tricks to part you from your money
quacks	sellers of fake cures	denigratory term for doctors, a ridiculous name making the idea of any scientific basis doubtful
faddists	people who follow fashion	slaves of any foolish fashion of the moment, embracing temporary enthusiasms

Commentary

If you included in your list any of the following words:

Word	Connotation
bulges	overflowing, superfluous fat
untidy grid	unattractive pattern of criss crosses, pitted, ugly
mud	sludge, wet, wobbly
oozing	flowing slowly, greasily

then you have not looked closely enough at the question you were asked. These words, although they certainly are emotive, are not about the morality of the 'cellulite business'; they are about 'cellulite' itself.

Answers – Word Choice further practice

B For each of the following words, your answer should move from the denotation through the connotations to show why the scientific, rational basis of many of these words creates an impression of trustworthiness.

Word	Denotation	Connotation
reputable	has a good reputation	respected, can be trusted
scientific	based upon verifiable evidence	suggests academic credibility beyond question
sound	well-grounded	solid, dependable
factual	based on fact	evidence-based therefore very reliable
invaluable	beyond price	worthy of the highest praise, of great importance
public service	assisting others	reliably performing a very important function in society
antidote	cure for a poison	here, reasoned oppositional argument

Commentary

In answering these questions based on quite simple vocabulary it is difficult for students to disentangle the denotations from the connotations but the effort of trying to see beyond the literal meanings to their power of suggestion makes the exercise worthwhile and should extend the scope of active vocabulary and range of expression. The fact that the answers above appear in table form is only to help you identify the various strands. It is not necessarily the best way of answering this kind of question in the exam.

Sentence Structure

'Decorating Should Come With a Health Warning' – questions begin on page 15

A (a) 'Believe me, you'll be noticed.' This short sentence forces itself into your attention by addressing you, the reader, in a critical way, implying that you would make a fool of yourself. It is an anti-climax that follows the climax of the previous sentence which is built up through 'fake' designer terms to a ridiculous level – 'post-retro (!) plastic flower'.

> ### Commentary
> When you are talking about the effect of a short sentence you should always identify the sentence either by quoting it (as in the previous answer) or by quoting its beginning and end to distinguish it from other short sentences in the vicinity. Any climax should also be clearly described. It is not enough to say simply that a climax has built up. You should specify what it is building up to – in this case a ridiculous concept, and ideally you should show some of the steps by which it gets there. Quoted above was 'post-retro plastic flower'. In itself this is a well chosen reference but it needs a comment to link it in with the sense of the ridiculous which is at the heart of the climax. The inverted commas round 'fake' show the artificiality and cheapness of the whole idea. Another aspect of the climax could have been identified through reference to 'stunned', to 'forced to gasp', or to 'daring reinterpretation'. The anti-climax here is the suggestion in 'be noticed' – that what you will be noticed for is being a bit stupid. 'Believe me' could equally well have been developed into an answer.

   (b) 'Lay down your nail-guns, good people.' This sentence is short, commanding, conclusive, memorable and aimed to stop people making fools of themselves by embarking on way-out decorative projects, clearly giving us the writer's point of view. Its structure is obviously a deliberate imitation of 'Lay down your guns', suggesting a crime movie, perhaps, with the playful implication that the whole activity is 'criminal'. The direct address at the end of the sentence, with its patronising 'good people', adds to the tone of slight mockery which has been apparent throughout the article.

Answers — Sentence Structure ✓

> **Commentary**
>
> The comment on tone requires both the quotation of the words or phrase which alert you to the mocking tone (as in 'good people') and the comment made through the adjective ('patronising').

B 'acres of blond-wood, angle-poised lamps and more MDF than you can shake a pulped stick at'

This list gives an impression of the amount and scale of DIY objects available and suggests these things are vulgarly common or too fashionable. The word 'acres' implies that all these items are about to swamp us in a sea of tat.

'19th–century bordellos, Scandinavian saunas and south-east Asian opium dens'

This series of parallel phrases suggests the immense variety and scope of such rooms but also emphasises the morally dubious, vaguely indecent nature of the rooms and builds to a ludicrous climax in 'opium dens'. All of this exaggerates the impression of the dreadful nature of the results.

> **Commentary**
>
> In the examples above the writer uses a tried and tested rhetorical technique effectively to influence you. Since Greek and Roman times orators have been aware that three is a magic number. They used the 'rule of three', sometimes called a triad, in their speeches.

Sentence Structure – further practice

'Junk Food' – questions begin on page 20

A (a) *Lines 5–8*

Each question is a minor sentence raising a serious issue like 'Iraq?' or 'Law and order?' as hinted at in paragraph 1: 'cataclysm'. The abruptness of each of these questions followed by the equally formulaic answers suggests the response is 'to order'.

The list of issues beginning 'Nuclear power' shows the range and extent of the problems which the world has to face, suggesting that there is no end nor any solution in sight.

The list could also be said to build up to a climax, 'truth and justice' being eternal, unchanging, fundamental, crucial, 'cataclysmic' issues. The length of this question prompts an answer which contains the idea of an ever-growing amount of information – 'volumes'. All three responses taken together give the impression that the amount written 'to order' is getting out of hand.

In the final brief sentence he self-deprecatingly adds himself to the roll of guilty parties because he is writing the article we are reading.

> **Commentary**
> There are at least four opportunities to answer here: questions, short sentence, listing, climax.

(b) *Lines 9–13*

The clause after the colon in line 11 is a summing up of, or climax to, what has gone before the colon. The two (appropriately?) short sentences 'Little things' and 'Small people' lead to the list of everyday happenings – 'Everyday conundrums...' – to provide a whole lot of domestic, ordinary family detail which is summed up by a statement which emphasises the fact that the mundane is important, 'what counts...'

> **Commentary**
> This use of the colon here is not the one most commonly found. It is more usual to have an initial statement which is then expanded or explained by what follows the colon. Here the detail is before the colon, and the part after the colon is the definitive, summing up statement.

(c) *Line 14*

'So' signals that this follows from the discussion in the previous paragraph about life's mundane-seeming trivialities here exemplified by the extremely trivial 'a bag of crisps'. 'If not, why not?' asks us to consider the questions we should be asking which are the subject of the next paragraph – why, for example, small treats are a big problem.

> **Commentary**
>
> The following formula can help with link questions. The part referring back is 'x' ('So ... crisps') and it refers back to 'x' ('mundane ... matters. Little things') in the previous paragraph; the part referring forward is 'y' (the two questions) and it refers forward to 'y' ('Why... Why...') in the paragraph which follows.

(d) *Lines 15–20*

The inverted commas round 'treat' in line 17 suggest that the word has not got its usual connotations of something nice – it is something nasty and dangerous. This adds to a puzzled or angry tone.

The parenthesis created by the dashes in lines 18 and 19 '– and spending...' suggests that there are people who profit out of advertising the stuff to children, who are in fact working hard at hurting children. This casual throwaway addition, marked by the dashes, suggests a cynical tone.

> **Commentary**
>
> The function of the inverted commas round 'treat' (where the 'niceness' of the thing is questioned) is different from the function of the inverted commas round 'stuffs' in line 26 which exacerbates an already critical term. Don't fall into the trap of thinking that the functions will always be the same.

(e) *Lines 21–25*

The balanced sentence 'The <u>latter</u>...; the <u>former</u>' shows how the two organisations were opposed. '<u>rules</u> that might <u>govern</u>' is shot down by 'the <u>proposals (rules)</u> were <u>inadequate</u>.'

(f) *Lines 26–30*

Inverted commas round 'stuffs' (separated from the term 'foodstuff') now suggest a derogatory description of the food – it is worthless.

Repetition of 'treated' suggests that these things surprisingly require careful handling like drugs and alcohol – the repetition underlines the danger of the foodstuffs.

The parenthesis marked by the pair of dashes in line 29 creates an aura of disbelief about the claim that all children will be in bed by 9p.m. This implies that they will, in fact, be exposed to dangerous advertising.

The list of adjectives describing treats in lines 29–30 exaggerates the damage that these treats can do by piling up a number of increasingly pejorative words – 'salty…' leading up to the most serious, 'addictive'.

(g) *Lines 31–37*

<u>When you</u> allow…' and '<u>when you</u> volunteer…': the repetition puts the blame fairly and squarely on the shoulders of the parent – 'you'. It further suggests that you don't just allow one thing, you go on to do more – endanger your child.

'so very large' and 'so very miserable': the repetition creates a parallel structure which leaves no doubt that the misery is caused by the largeness.

'Why' and 'And why' are followed by two alternative answers – the structure is similar and throws into prominence the difference – one bad ('drugged units') and one good ('healthy…delight').

Repetition of 'because' at the beginning of all three sentences highlights the different answers – one negative ('drugged …bovine'), one positive ('healthy… delight'); and the <u>third</u> time shifts it to a new dimension, a summary (the climax): the beauty of life; too precious to waste.

Information and Evidence

'Sinking London' – questions begin on page 23

A   In this answer the following 'codes' have been used to identify each aspect:

signposts are underlined

illustrations are in italics

expansions have wavy underlining

definitions are in bold

Lines 19–36
<u>So why</u> is the south of England sinking?

<u>First,</u> the burden of Scottish ice pushed up the crust in surrounding areas that were ice-free, *just as pressing down on one part of a water bed makes adjacent areas of it rise*. That process is <u>now</u> in reverse: the <u>once</u>-raised regions of Southern England and the southern Baltic are now sinking.

<u>Secondly,</u> sea level is rising worldwide. <u>Once</u> it rose rapidly as the ice sheets over places like Scotland melted. <u>Now</u> global warming may be melting glaciers, sending more melt-water into the oceans. As the oceans grow warmer, thermal expansion <u>also</u> raises sea level.

<u>Thus</u> the south of England gets a double whammy – sinking crust and rising sea level. <u>And</u> the London area is subjected to a quintuple whammy. <u>Apart from</u> the two factors already mentioned, the Thames Valley is a syncline, **an area of locally subsided crust**. <u>Also,</u> until recently groundwater extracted from below London was causing further subsidence. <u>Finally,</u> the funnel shape of the North Sea tends to bank up storm surges to ever greater heights as they enter the Thames Estuary.

<u>All this</u> adds up to one inescapable fact: the lower Thames was not a good place to site a major capital city.

B   (a) The earth's surface layer is pliable enough to allow it to sink or rise depending on the mass placed on it (in this case the weight of ice).

> **Commentary**
> There is no point in trying to find other words for such simple terms as 'sinking and rising'.

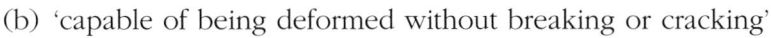

Answers – Information and Evidence

(b) 'capable of being deformed without breaking or cracking'

The context gives the contrast of 'is not rigid' with 'but very slightly elastic' showing that 'elastic' in this context must mean the opposite of 'rigid'.

> **Commentary**
> This question asks for two things:
>
> - the **meaning** of the word – definition
> - and **context**: how you arrived at it – here by contrast with its opposite.

(c) The illustration about making a boat float higher in the water when you remove the cargo is an everyday familiar concept. It helps the reader to realise that that is what is happening on a very large scale when the weight of the ice is removed from the surface of Britain.

> **Commentary**
> The purpose of an illustration is usually to simplify. Here the simplification comes because the writer takes a small scale example to illustrate a large scale problem.

(d) time taken

amount of uplift

> **Commentary**
> 'Briefly' in this question means briefly. The skill needed is the ability to summarise, by reducing the paragraph to its essence.

(e) The process can be seen within a lifetime in the northern Baltic region.

Or (more obviously)

In the north east of Scotland there are signs of previous beaches several metres above sea level.

Answers – Information and Evidence

(f) • This sentence sets up the topic for the second half of the passage: what is happening in London.

• It reminds the reader of the title.

• It asks a question which the reader has the expectation will be answered.

• The single line paragraph gives weight and impact to the question by isolating it.

• The use of 'So' shows that the question is dependent on the statements which have gone before.

• It acts as a linking sentence between the description of what is happening in the north of Scotland, which fills the first half of the article, and the description of what is happening or will happen to the south of England: the subject of the second half of the passage.

> ### Commentary
> There are six suggestions for an answer here. Obviously there is no time to write all six answers in the time you are given; and there is no need to. One really satisfactory answer like the first one or the last one would be enough. Remember to tailor your answer to the number of marks awarded for it.
>
> Remember also that merely to write down:
>
> *topic sentence / title / single line paragraph / the use of 'So'/ acts as a link*
>
> will gain no marks at all. These are merely identifications without any comment to show how they are linked to the question about the effectiveness of the sentence.

(g) Southern England is now sinking because the loss of ice in Scotland is letting Scotland rise, so that England tips down.

There is more water in the sea caused by melting ice/global warming.

Answers – Information and Evidence ✓

> **Commentary**
>
> You are asked to 'summarise'. This means that your answer should at least be shorter than the original. The main point, or idea, is what is wanted. You should also try to put your answer in your own words even though in this case you have not been specifically asked to do so. (Remember there is a general instruction on the front of the exam paper about using your own words whenever possible.)

(h) • England is tipping down towards the south.

• Levels of water rising in the sea.

• The Thames Valley is on a part of the earth's surface which is going down even more than the surrounding area.

• Too much water taken from the earth below London.

• Strong tides and winds can force the water level to pile up when it gets into the Thames Estuary.

> **Commentary**
>
> You are asked to 'list'. You are not being asked for explanations. You want to get your answer down quickly and succinctly. You are also asked this time to do so in your own words as far as possible. 'Sea', 'water' and 'estuary' obviously can be repeated – there is nothing difficult about these words. But you should not write down 'in a syncline' or 'area of locally subsided crust' because this would not show that you have understood these words. You have merely 'lifted' them out of the passage and put them in your answer and you would get no marks for that item. Similarly you should not 'lift' 'bank up storm surges' – you should 'translate' the phrase to show that you have understood what the problem for London is.

Answers – Information and Evidence

(i)   In terms of ideas this is a good conclusion because it sums up in one sentence the danger that London is in – which was the subject suggested by the title.

In terms of style it is a good way to conclude the passage because:

- The sentence structure leads up to a climax after the initial statement 'the inescapable fact'.

- The word choice of 'inescapable' suggests the inevitability of the end for London.

- The colon which follows 'fact' leads into an identification of the fact – in this case that London is in the wrong place.

- This climactic idea is also pointed up because there is a slightly humorous tone – as if the original inhabitants of London should have thought of all these things before they built the first house!

Commentary

If the code for this question is 'E', then the answer above, which deals with both ideas and style, is required.

If the code for the question is U/E, then the question is asking you specifically to deal with the ideas of the passage.

If the code for the question is A/E, then the question is asking you to deal with the style of the writing – in other words it is an analysis question and you are looking at aspects of language: sentence structure, climax, word choice, tone. . .

Information and Evidence – further practice

'History of Bathing' – questions begin on page 26

A In Greece; in Rome; in the Middle Ages; in the eighteenth and nineteenth centuries; from about 1860; with the coming of...

> **Commentary**
> The last of these is the least obvious but it moves the time on to the present day.

B (a) For the Romans the 'meaning' is physical pleasure/enjoyment; the 'purpose' is maintaining the fabric of society; the 'method' is using hot and cold water.

(b) *Lines 10–16*

- For Greeks a bath was for fitness and exercise.

- For Romans it was to enjoy and be soothed into a state of feeling refreshed.

- For both Greeks and Romans it was a social occasion, not just for hygiene.

Lines 17–24

- In mediaeval times public baths still provided a community function.

- For mediaeval monks it was more to do with hygiene and definitely not for pleasure.

- At other times baths have been seen as useful to soothe the mind and spirit.

- In the eighteenth and nineteenth centuries bathing was seen mainly as a cure for illness.

Lines 25–29

- After 1860 baths were strictly for cleanliness, not pleasure, being of cold water.

- Today, with the availability of hot water, bathing is for cleanliness and pleasure.

C (a) The priests scared people by making the water sacred – the property of the gods – and promising divine punishment to anyone who contaminated a water source. As a result these water sources were regarded with respect and kept pure for bathing.

(b) sources, springs and pools/sacred bathing rites

Structure of an Argument

'Elephants and Revenge' – questions begin on page 31

A *A Paragraph 3 (lines 13–16)*

(a) <u>Or rather,</u> <u>because</u> they do not like humans. As <u>one researcher</u> <u>reports</u> from India, elephants left to their own devices in remote areas tend to be <u>placid and tolerant.</u> <u>On the other hand,</u> 'the <u>more</u> human beings they see, the <u>less</u> <u>tolerant</u> they become'.

(b) 'Or rather' links back to the ideas of the previous paragraph and is going to contradict the idea, that there was no motive. The motive which is now being introduced is that they did not like humans, as the evidence of their intolerance shows.

(c) On their own they are gentle and 'tolerant'; near human beings they become nasty. The contrast is made clear by '<u>on the other hand</u>' which highlights the contrast between <u>placid and tolerant</u> (without human company) and <u>less tolerant</u> (when human beings are near).

> ### Commentary
> Other points to notice about this paragraph are that 'Or rather' is powerfully positioned by the paragraph break as well as by the fact that the sentence has been 'broken'. It suggests that their dislike of humans was the real and more important motive. '<u>One researcher reports</u>' is preparing us for the evidence for this idea.

B *Paragraph 4 (lines 17–21)*

(a) <u>Given</u> mankind's <u>record</u> in dealing with other species, you can't blame the elephants for <u>that</u>. They are not stupid creatures and their memories are <u>indeed</u> good enough to allow them to remember acts of cruelty and violence. <u>In other words</u>, they have motive. <u>Add</u> opportunity and you have what homo sapiens would call <u>revenge.</u>

(b) The phrase 'mankind's record' at the beginning of the sentence refers **forward** to the mention of cruelty and violence; the 'that' at the end of the sentence refers **back** to the behaviour of the elephants mentioned in the previous paragraph – 'the less tolerant...'

(c) '<u>In other words</u>' suggests a summing up or an explanation of the part of the paragraph beforehand. It catalogues the harms which mankind has done to elephants. This is evidence for their 'motive.

Answers – Structure of an Argument ✓

> **Commentary**
> The answer to (b) illustrates the reversed form of the link
> sentence. More usually the first item in the sentence refers back
> and the second idea refers forward. There is a further
> explanation of this in the commentary on question (c) on page
> 64 and on paragraph 4(a) on page 75. Another point to notice
> about this paragraph is that by using '<u>Given</u>' (motive) and '<u>Add</u>'
> (the opportunity) the writer is providing a 'recipe' for '<u>revenge</u>'.

C *Paragraph 5 (lines 22–32)*

(a) <u>If that is so</u>, the <u>questions</u> come thick and fast. Creatures capable of
bearing a grudge <u>surely</u> possess the elements of what we, of all
animals, would recognise as a society. <u>Haven't we spent</u> millennia
regarding ourselves as the <u>only</u> beasts capable of understanding the
idea <u>of revenge</u>? <u>So what do we</u> actually understand by the word?
With all due respect to the raging bull elephants, it must involve some
<u>fairly primitive emotion</u>: the elephants <u>are not writing letters</u> to the
press demanding an apology from the Ugandan people, after all; they
<u>are, in fact, attacking</u> humans aggressively. <u>If</u> these reports are <u>reliable</u>,
<u>we</u> have a <u>lesson</u> on our hands. <u>Even</u> among the elephants, the desire
for revenge is born of pain, trauma, and cruelty. <u>And</u> is that not <u>even
more so</u> in our own species which seems wedded to revenge?

(b) 'If that is so,' links back to the proposition that the elephants
experience the desire for revenge and looks forward to the
'questions' about the concept of revenge and the need to define it.

(c) The colon after the phrase 'fairly primitive emotion:' prepares us for
an expansion of this idea. It is expanded in two parts separated by a
semi-colon: the first expansion humorously suggests the reaction will
not be a sophisticated one – 'they (the elephants) are not writing
letters' (a peaceful protest, a civilised emotion). The second
expansion after the semi-colon suggests their actual reaction – 'they
are, in fact, attacking' (a violent protest, an uncivilised emotion).

(d) 'If these reports are reliable' parallels 'If that is so' to highlight the
important shift in the ideas in the article – which move the behaviour
from the elephants to the humans.

(e) The word 'Even' suggests that, surprisingly, where you would not
expect it (among the elephants) the desire for revenge is caused by
maltreatment. So when you reach the next sentence beginning with
'And' followed by 'even more so' the inevitability of revenge as a
human emotion is highlighted and the argument strengthened.

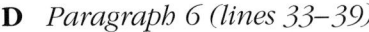

Answers – Structure of an Argument

D *Paragraph 6 (lines 33–39)*

(a) <u>Such revenge</u> may represent a primitive emotion, but <u>that emotion</u> has destructive power. The <u>disease</u> is an ancient, global pandemic. <u>Like</u> Uganda's elephants <u>we</u> could <u>all</u> probably stand a psycho-therapeutic course in anger management. The <u>common feature</u>, the unlikely <u>connection</u>, is that the destructive pachyderms <u>first</u> had to be <u>victimised</u> <u>before</u> they could feel a <u>need for victims</u>. There is not a human society on the planet that does not claim the <u>same excuse</u>.

(b) The first four words encapsulate the two threads of the argument in a juxtaposition that throws weight on its surprising unexpectedness: elephants actually share a trait with us, although we thought it was unique to humans. This link is emphasised by 'common feature' and 'connection' and the 'victimised/need for victims' point is shown to be weak in the case of both the elephants and humans by the use of the final words of the passage 'same excuse'. It's not a reason, merely an excuse.

> **Commentary**
>
> The other important point to notice about this paragraph is the first sentence, which creates a link in exactly the same way as the one in line 6. 'Such revenge' links back to the revenge being discussed in the previous paragraph and 'that emotion has a destructive power' is expanded on in the next sentence about the problem, which he is now labelling a 'disease', showing how destructive and widespread the effects of revenge are and always have been throughout human society.
>
> In the second half of the article the writer deliberately refers to human beings in a zoological way – 'homo sapiens', 'species' and 'beasts' – in such a way as to strengthen his comparison between humans and elephants.

Structure of an Argument – further practice

'Classroom With a View' – questions begin on page 35

A *Paragraph 1 (lines 1–6)*

(a) Architecturally – attractive, uplifting; environmentally sympathetic (made of natural materials); drawing from the best of both old and new traditions.

(b) Sense of community; where children want to be ('village' and 'long').

Paragraph 2 (lines 7–15)

(a) Ladakh has a better situation with a wonderful view ('location' and 'aesthetics').

British school is ugly; urban surroundings suggest a sense of deprivation ('ring roads' etc., 'battling', 'rundown').

(b) Not a place where teachers and children want to be.

Paragraph 3 (lines 16–22)

(a) 'If … then… even if.' 'If …then…even if'.

(b) If new schools are to be no more than factories for exam passing they will fail to create a worthwhile society.

If they aim to make children creative with an urge to learn (for the sake of it) they will succeed in doing so.

(c) The architecture is actually irrelevant.

Paragraph 4 (lines 23–32)

(a) 'School with a soul' ('x') links back to the description of 'good' schools which inspire pupils ('x') in the previous paragraph; and 'welcoming' ('y') refers on to the rest of the paragraph which describes a school being made welcoming ('y').

> ### Commentary
> The following formula can help with link questions. The part referring back is 'x' and it refers back to 'x' in the previous paragraph; the part referring forward is 'y' and it refers forward to 'y' in the paragraph which follows.

(b) The anecdote gives the reader a concrete example which shows how powerful an architectural change can be. He describes an incident where an architect transformed a dark, confined, ugly building which produced bad behaviour into a place full of light with a pleasant centre for communal activity simply by roofing over a courtyard.

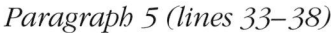

Answers – Structure of an Argument further practice

Paragraph 5 (lines 33–38)

(a) A contrast is made between a good school as being a place for enjoyment and a bad resembling an assembly line.

(b) The writer sees Britain as being fundamentally focused on money-making and seeing education as a way of producing obedient workers for the economy.

(c) 'Machines' is developed by 'hard', 'shiny' and 'cogs'; and the idea is that he sees the system reducing education to a soulless mechanistic procedure for producing functional 'parts' – the workers. He uses these harsh images of a factory process to persuade us that the system is unfriendly and inhumane.

Paragraph 6 (lines 39–42)

(a) 'Perhaps' picks up both the insidious implications of '<u>surely</u>' in the previous paragraph and the idea of British schools as <u>needing</u> to be machines.

'Perhaps <u>not</u>' states his point of view clearly. He disagrees with that view and goes on to restate his own.

(b) The word 'village' reminds the reader of his praise for Ladakh in the opening paragraph, and the anecdote about improvements in Southwark – both of which reflect his own preference for a welcoming cooperative community.

The word 'factory' obviously refers back to the machines and cogs of the education system he does not like (in paragraphs 3 and 5).

'Confronted one another' is a reminder of a situation without the necessary welcoming properties which he feels that architecture can help to provide (paragraph 4).

'Everyone might enjoy' is a summing up of the point he is making throughout, that education can be enjoyable and uplifting rather than merely utilitarian.

The final words 'Southwark or Ladakh' refer back to the two places which have been the subject of the article and which now have acquired some symbolic significance.

Imagery

'Summit Fever' – questions begin on page 39

A 'A straight green line slashed as if by a razor' gives the impression that the channel for the water looks unnaturally carved, as if some giant hand had used a razor blade to cut the hillside. It suggests precision and power, a deliberate assault – all of which adds to the sense of scale and harshness the writer is aware of.

'lifeline of water'. Lifeline suggests a rope cast out to save a person in difficulties and, in carrying on the idea that the water is necessary to the fertility and plant life of the area, stresses the precarious and fragile nature of the vital connection provided by the slim trickle of water from the hillside to the village.

B (a) 'loped along'. This gives the impression of the path being like an animal such as a wolf (appropriate to the wilderness). It suggests an easy sinuous kind of movement, as if the path was taking its time getting where it wanted to go – and possibly its route being dictated by the terrain through which it was travelling. This is a natural image stressing a sense of the domination of the landscape over human activity.

(b) 'It was a network as complex and organic as the circulation of the blood, divided similarly into main arteries, veins, capillaries'. This image continues the idea of the importance of water and the irrigation channels to the life of the villages. The comparison with the circulation system of the human body – arteries, veins and capillaries – gives a graphic description of the complexity of the 'network' from larger, into medium, into smaller channels, feeding even the remotest of the hundred fields. It stresses the writer's wonder at, and appreciation of, the hand of man in taming the wilderness.

(c) 'new tack'. This image suggests that the course of the water changed suddenly, as when a sailing boat suddenly changes its course with respect to the wind (in response to the repositioning of sails) and darts off in a new direction. Here it adds to the unexpectedness of the change of direction, as a new channel is opened and allows the water to charge off to do 'good' somewhere else. Again this stresses the writer's wonder at the ingenuity of man's manipulation of nature.

Answers – Imagery

> **Commentary**
>
> 'New tack' is a sailing term, so the answer must contain some sense of the literal sailing manoeuvre.
>
> The application of the term to the irrigation channels allows the writer to use the shared connotations of sharpness and speed to express the unexpectedness of the change in direction of the water in a graphic way.
>
> The last sentence of the answer above fulfils the remaining task of relating this to the writer's experience/emotions/perceptions.
>
> Together, these three elements constitute a fully developed answer to this kind of question.

(d) 'the great peaks stood frozen to attention'. Here we have an example of personification, although, of course, it is also a kind of metaphor. The great peaks are not literally standing to attention. The writer is seeing them as soldiers, drawn up stiff and tall, waiting for something – further orders, the end of the world, the onslaught by climbers? In any case the impression of a cold, frozen, overwhelming series of mountains is highlighted by the image which adds to the writer's sense of anticipation, and possibly fear.

(e) 'I was an arrow, moving further and further away from the tension that set me going, getting nearer and nearer my destination.' What we are dealing with here is a metaphor. It is not 'true' that he was 'an arrow'. What is suggested by the arrow/tension idea is that all the preparation, anticipation, and potential of the writer for climbing these peaks is now being put to use and allowed expression, just as the tension in the bow-string lends energy and movement to an arrow. There is also the idea that the arrow will move directly and quickly to its target, as the writer wants to move swiftly towards his goal – the mountain.

Answers – Imagery

Commentary

The answer to (e) starts with the application of the arrow/bowstring idea to the central feeling of potential energy directed single-mindedly at the mountains.

The answer then links it to the literal concept of a tensed bowstring and the sense of its potential power released into the arrow in flight.

The writer's feelings of excitement and anticipation are already included within the body of the answer and continued in the statement of the writer's goal in the last sentence.

These three elements, although in a different order from question (c), constitute a fully developed answer.

Imagery – further practice

'Women of the Year Awards' – questions begin on page 41

A   (a) Metaphor: 'training their lenses…straight'

        Simile: 'as big and black as a hole in outer space'

  (b) Metaphor: the long lenses at the ends of the cameras are aiming straight at her as the barrels of guns are trained on their target, leaving her feeling as if she is under attack. This suggests a sense of intimidation in what ought to be a glamorous situation.

        Simile: the round lenses seem so intimidating and vast that they almost seem likely to suck her into them as black holes suck in all matter close to them in the universe, adding to her unease. The astronomical difference in scale suggests an intense terror.

  (c) The long, narrow strip of red carpet is being compared to the long plank of wood on which pirates' victims were made to walk to their deaths as punishment. Again the sense of being in a scary place is emphasised by the deathly connotations of 'walking the plank'. The use of the glamorous adjective 'crimson' for the plank intensifies the incongruity and adds to the aptness of the metaphor.

        The following simile 'lights on top as blinding as the Caribbean sun' shows the lights as being hurtful in their intensity, in the same way that looking at the sun is painful. The fact that it is a Caribbean sun fits with the metaphor relating to the pirates, as they are thought of as being based in the Caribbean in former times.

  (d) The simile suggests that Naomi Campbell's limbs are long and angular and terribly thin, like long straight knitting needles; and the 'thrown up a close' part suggests that the contortions of the limbs in various poses were like a bundle of mismatched knitting needles which had landed in an untidy heap. The attitude of the writer is that she is unimpressed by the physical attributes of the model and the homely, derogatory reference to 'up a close' suggests commonness or vulgarity.

> ### Commentary
> This is a long simile and to answer the question fully it would be necessary to comment on the effectiveness of each part of the comparison. This answer deals with: selection, knitting needles, thrown, close. An acceptable answer, however, need not deal with all the components.

Answers — Imagery further practice

(e) 'Into a newborn nebula of flashbulbs exploding in infinity' suggests that around the model there was excitement and admiration, with everyone enthused by their glimpse of the celebrity. The astronomical connotations of the intensity of the light and its vast extent suggest the amount of media attention. The comparison to a new star being born is hyperbolic, but is symptomatic of the excitement which celebrities create.

The comparison between the 'black hole' which greeted the writer on her entrance and the 'newborn nebula' which greeted Campbell points up the contrast between their status in this world.

(f) • 'bitching' suggests snapping, nipping as if small animals were engaged in a petty squabble

• 'back-stabbing' suggests using words as weapons treacherously behind people's backs

• 'torch-tongued jealousy' suggests tongues seen as flames of a fiercely burning torch used to scorch reputations in envy

• 'blanket (outbreak)' suggests that they all act like each other, like sheep, in an unthinking manner

• 'sisterly solidarity' would normally suggest the sort of cohesion among a group usually reserved for serious political situations, usually applied to women standing shoulder to shoulder but here being used sarcastically, with 'sisterly' suggesting a closeness of relationship which is not convincing.

(g) The idea that all these glamorous women applauded a speech which stated that the only thing they had in common was that they would all die (!) suggests a rather simplistic bird-brained reaction, which is furthered by the use of 'riotously' suggesting a reaction influenced by a crowd mentality. It is a final 'put down' by the writer of the whole idea of the 'Glamorous Woman' celebrity culture.

Tone

'Winnie the Pooh' – questions begin on page 45

A   Sound or sentence structure or juxtaposition:

'He's overweight and over-rated'. The repetition of 'over' in these phrases carries on the critical tone of the previous descriptions of Pooh's size by suggesting the idea of excess, but there is a humorous juxtaposition of 'overweight' which is a physical thing and 'over-rated' which is an abstract or judgmental idea. By treating the two phrases as if they were exactly the same, an incongruity is created which makes for a humorous outcome. So the tone created by the repetition of the sound or structure, and the juxtaposition, is again humorously critical or mocking.

Register:

The use of colloquial and slangy phrases like 'fat chance', 'thick, greedy' and 'backside' – down-to-earth, common English insults – creates a humorous tone because they appear in the middle of what could at least be pretending to be a serious article.

Sentence structure/punctuation:

The use of a question, 'When did you ever see him do a bit of exercise?' This is a rhetorical question. You are expected to agree with the writer in her opinion that 'ages ago' or 'never' would be the correct answer to the question. The writer is using the question to align the reader with her ideas because she is pushing the reader to agree with her in mocking the bear.

Note: These are not the only answers which exist for Question A, but they are the most obvious.

B   The dignified, formal register of the first sentence with words like 'ardent', 'chronic' and 'merchandise' contrasts abruptly with the insultingly humorous 'grubby paws' in the next sentence.

The image, 'grubby paws all over the mass market', suggests that Pooh has literally put his paw marks on all the goods in the marketplace and contaminated them with his own marking (probably honey); figuratively it suggests the infiltration of the market and the impossibility of anyone being able to ignore the concept of the bear. It suggests that the market has been perverted in Pooh's favour (producing a critical tone) but at the same time the idea of 'grubby paws' is colloquial and quite funny, making the overall impression less serious – leading to a tone of mockery.

Answers – Tone ✓

The alliteration of 'podgy profile' gives the idea of a kind of small explosion of disgust represented by the repeated 'p' sound. It again suggests dislike for his plumpness, but the phrase itself has a catchy rhythm. The incongruity of the formal word, 'profile', (usually thought of as a sharp distinguished angle of view), being juxtaposed with 'podgy' (a basic English word suggesting shapeless and flabby) creates humour. The alliteration therefore contributes to the mocking tone of the article.

C 'So do us all a favour, Pooh, and follow suit.'

The use of 'so' suggests a tone of finality – it's the undeniable conclusion which the writer has reached. The use of 'all' suggests that she feels she has succeeded in winning her audience round to her way of thinking – we **all** want rid of Pooh. The positioning and use of commas to isolate Pooh's name, addressing him directly, adds to a tone of 'sweet reasonableness' on the part of the writer. She thinks he'll be persuaded to do as she says: 'follow suit' – a definite invitation to depart.

Tone – further practice

'The Olympics' – questions begin on page 48

A (a) Atmosphere: abandoned, desolate, unattractive, industrial, wasteland

- 'grey-green' gives the desolate feeling of a green that is lifeless cold, dead

- 'brutalist (skyline)' suggests a crude angular and bulky (skyline), primitive and unattractive

- 'thumped' implies punched thus creating a sense of brutal collision

- 'low cloud cover' would be oppressive, dreary, claustrophobic

- 'rusty (oil bowsers)' suggests an area of rundown decay

- '(industrial) hugger-mugger' suggests chaotic piles of assorted junk abandoned or secreted in factory yards

(b) Mood of depression/gloom: 'grimly'

(c) *Imagery*
'sacrifice on the altar of "sporting excellence"': literally – killing an animal for religious reasons, to pacify the god whose altar it is; metaphorically – destroying a football pitch, in the name of 'sporting excellence' which thus seems to be elevated to the status of a god, having more significance than it deserves. This is therefore adding to the critical derogatory tone by suggesting that the proposed tarmac will destroy something good without any gain.

Punctuation
Inverted commas round the catch phrase 'sporting excellence' show that the writer feels this phrase to be not worth-while, not important enough, or not excellent enough, to cause the destruction. It adds to the derogatory tone, as he is lifting out this phrase in a disbelieving or disgusted way.

Sentence structure
The use of parenthesis – 'a local...national pride' – gives the definition of 'this sacrifice' in simpler words so that the reader can sense his disbelief at the stupidity of destroying sporting facilities.

'Take it from me' is an emphatic introduction to the important dismissive statement which follows; it allows no disagreement.

Parenthesis – 'Britain as a whole' – suggests the scale of the resulting fiasco will affect much more than London – we needn't think we will be exempt from the fallout; we needn't feel superior.

'None of . . .' plus the colon, prepares us for a number of items which will *not* come about, and the list builds up to a grand climax starting from the 'fitness of the inhabitants' to the improvement in the financial standing of the nation. The impossibility of all these things happening adds to the tone of despair reflecting his feeling that nothing will come of it.

(d) 'On the contrary' helps to structure the argument at this point in the article as it moves to provide the balance between what the Olympics *won't* do (any of the achievements wished for in the previous paragraph) and what they *will* do (all the disasters foreseen in this paragraph).

The sentence contributes to the tone of the article by means of the list of negative results starting from the financial disaster up to the future of expensive recrimination which will go on well into the future. The nature of the climax is highlighted by the length of clause given to each of the drawbacks, the most lengthy and worst being kept to the end. The relentless nature of the list of disasters allows no room for any lightening of the despairing tone.

(e) The change in register is from the more formal-sounding adulatory terms of 'sycophant', and 'Great Leader' (capitalized) which create a sense of heavy irony, to the more directly insulting 'moron'. This has the effect of putting down the participants and intensifying the hostile and disrespectful tone of the writer.

> ### Commentary
> Look at the section on page 8 about Writer's Point of View. Note that, in this passage, as in the passage on Surveillance by Jonathan Raban, there is no counter-argument offered. As a discerning reader, you will realise that you are being very much bludgeoned into taking the same point of view on the Olympics as Will Self.

(f) • Formal: 'guarantee', 'legacy', 'delusion', 'decade'

    • Informal: 'flog off', 'gay abandon'

Answers – Tone further practice ✓

> ### Commentary
> You are rarely asked simply to quote from a passage without any comment, but where you are asked simply to quote, just do so.

(g) *Ideas*

The last sentence rounds off the passage by asserting that after all the fuss of the Olympics, and all the 'improvements', this part of London will still be just as depressing as it is portrayed at the start of the article.

Style

The word choice, imagery and structure of this sentence all enhance the overall critical tone of the article.

Word choice

- 'roust out' suggests to stir up/disrupt and create violent upheaval of lives for no good reason

- 'urban detritus' – the ugly rubbish generated by a city that is not so easily got rid of

- 'tumbling back' suggests rolling back (tumble weed) in a fast unstoppable movement negating all the effort

- 'throw (at it)' implies attempting to defeat by indiscriminate, desperate means which won't work

Imagery

'tidy the urban detritus under their magic finance carpet'.

This literally means sweeping the litter and rubbish out of sight under the carpet.

Metaphorically it means hiding all the nastier aspects of urban life, like left over industrial waste, for example, by means of paying lots of money for it to disappear as if by magic. There is also an allusion to the Arabian Nights' 'magic carpet' which is the way of escape.

It expresses the superficiality and temporary nature of the solution that the Olympics would bring. It adds to his **gloomy tone** by suggesting that there is no permanent benefit at all to the population of London – it's all show and window dressing, which will provide nothing permanent. It will be a costly operation providing nothing.

'Steely weeds' suggests almost that the weeds are so strong that they are not vegetable in origin at all; that they are as strong as steel and just as indestructible. It also is including under the heading of 'weeds' not just the actual vegetation, but the other things that can encroach on an untidy urban landscape like travellers' encampments and metal litter. Again these images add to the **critical tone** because it suggests the impossibility of anything preventing the return of the less pleasant aspects of the area.

Structure

The sentence balances around the word 'but'. The attempts which are made to improve the area are listed in the first part of the sentence. After the 'but' there is another group of factors which will negate all the attempts that have been made. The anti-climactic sequence of 'god, men or even planners can throw at it' brings the ineradicable permanence of ugly London to the forefront and leaves a picture of something too obstinate to be prettied up and given a makeover. The triad gives an extra sense of inevitability. These structures maintain the **bitter, derogatory tone** right to the last words of the article.

Commentary

It is worth noting that in the last two answers (on imagery and structure) wherever the word tone is used an attempt is made to specify a particular tone, like gloomy, critical, bitter, derogatory. All of these words are infinitely better than 'negative' or 'positive' which are very bland and non-specific.

Exaggeration

'Secret Life of Handbags' – questions begin on page 51

A (a) '394 days...56 weeks is nothing compared with the amount of time I do waste...'

The mock comic precision of 394 days combined with the picture 'sitting on the lavatory' sets up a sense of ridiculousness right from the start. The idea that *even* 56 weeks (*392* days) is *less* than the time that he waits for his wife to get the keys out, creates a ridiculous sense of disproportion and exaggeration reinforcing an affectionately derisory tone.

(b) 'A letter...is quicker...'

The idea that a letter, which at its quickest will take 24 hours, would be faster is incongruous because you compare in your mind's eye the journey the letter would make as compared with the eternal scrabbling about in the handbag. Telephones are, after all, supposed to make for instant communication. This exaggeration reinforces the tone of amused mockery.

(c) 'Stannah stairlift and some incontinence pads...'

His reaction moves into the realms of fantasy. A Stannah stairlift is obviously a large bulky fixed object the size of which is totally disproportionate to a handbag, and both the Stannah lift and the incontinence pads suggest the onset of extreme old age and infirmity, which obviously extends even further the length of time involved, reinforcing a wildly mocking and mildly insulting tone.

(d) 'Bones of Shergar'

Shergar was a race horse which was kidnapped in 1983 causing an enormous media furore. Nothing of him has ever been found despite the longest and most exacting search ever mounted for an animal. Therefore the idea that his large bones might be in the depths of the handbag creates a comic picture of objects of an incongruous size which have impossibly managed to evade the most rigorous search ever. This mocks the infinite capacity of the handbag.

'A secret pocket ... used by Lord Lucan ...'

Lord Lucan disappeared in 1974 suspected of the murder of his children's nanny. Again an intensive worldwide search over the last 30 years has produced no results in spite of numerous 'sightings'.

Answers – Exaggeration ✓

The idea that he might be contained in 'a secret pocket' suggests that the depths of the handbag are more inaccessible than the remotest corner of the world which might be sheltering Lord Lucan. The disparity of distance and size creates a comic picture – and 'secret' suggests that there are parts of her handbag which even his wife knows nothing about.

> **Commentary**
> The most useful technique to describe the operation of the fantasy which Clarkson is now indulging in is the notion of incongruity – the mismatch (disparity) of scale and the creation of a ridiculous 'picture' of cartoon-like disproportion.

B   'crust', 'asthenosphere', 'upper mantle', 'core'

All these words refer in geological terms to the interior of planet earth. Exaggeration is continued in the comparison between the size of handbag and the earth – a whole planet – which has the capacity to contain an infinity of objects. Each layer of the earth's formation from the outer crust – in this case represented presumably by the leather of the handbag itself – down to the inner core is giving the impression of yet another layer of out-of-date rubbish in the handbag. The cleverness of this development of ultimate disparity in size is that it parallels the journey into the heart of the handbag with a Journey to the Centre of the Earth.

Exaggeration – further practice

'Obesity Report Cards' – questions begin on page 52

A   *Lines 6–7*
'As soon as anyone can find one' exaggerates the scarcity of nurses by suggesting that there are no nurses to be found.

Lines 8–14
'Whole cities in Scotland that contain only fat people' exaggerates the percentage of the population which is fat and creates a mind-boggling image.

'Where you can waddle for days' exaggerates the duck-like gait of the fat and the interminable search for a thinner person.

'Anybody weighing less than 20st' exaggerates the weight of the population.

Lines 15–18
'Now too wide to get through the school gates' exaggerates the size of even an obese child – given the normal width of school gates.

'The little crane that hoists you off the sofa and heaves you about the house' exaggerates the immobility of the obese.

Line 19
'Spherical warm thing' exaggerates the shape of the fat child and perhaps a lack of care for him as a child.

B   An obvious answer is that the target is the parent who lets her child become obese. A more subtle answer is that the target is the SNP (or politicians generally) who come up with ineffectual ideas to deal with lifestyle problems.

Part Two

Comparative Evaluation Examples

Introduction

The final question (or questions), in which a comparison between the passages is asked for, is not easy. Under exam conditions, it has to be done in a very limited time – and it comes on top of all the effort you've already had to put into answering around 20 Close Reading questions. What's more, your mind may already be starting to shift to the Critical Essay paper!

Nevertheless, there are usually at least five marks to be gained, and the task involves what many people would argue is the most useful skill tested in Close Reading: the ability to take an overview of two pieces of writing and to make an informed comparison, supported by appropriate evidence.

Preparing and practising for this part of the paper is not easy either. A diet of 'past papers' alone will mean that you come to the task already fatigued from the effort of answering the preceding questions, and probably fed up with passages by this stage. On the other hand, attempting comparison exercises on their own has to be done without the 'advantage' of having worked through all the earlier questions, which are – or should have been – designed to assist your understanding of each writer's line of thought and appreciation of her/his style of writing.

The work in this section is designed to give you a range of opportunities to develop the important skills needed for comparing passages.

The Sets of passages are probably best worked through in order, since a reasonable amount of 'support' is given in the early ones, but this decreases steadily as the examples progress.

It is by no means essential to tackle all the tasks as formal 'tests'. Indeed, many of the passages and pairing of passages will benefit from general discussion before, during and after dealing with the questions. They have been selected as likely to be of interest to Higher English students and should provide plenty to talk about as well as (or maybe instead of) digging into the minutiae of sentence structure.

Each Set ends with at least one formal exam-type question, and most have some preparatory questions to help bridge the gap between having answered 45 marks' worth of questions on the passages already and approaching the comparison completely 'cold'. If you are going to get the most out of these exercises, allocation of time should not be rigid – allow yourself time to develop the skills (and appreciate the passages). In a formal 90-minute exam, you are not, realistically, going to be able to give much more than 12–15 minutes to the last question, but it would be a waste to try to do all the ones in this book in a mad rush.

Before you start, here are a few Dos and Don'ts for Comparison Questions:

DO

- Pay very careful attention to the **exact wording of the question** – this sounds a bit obvious, but a lot of students seem to think all comparison questions are the same and are just a general invitation to compare the passages. They are NOT; they may look similar, but every one is different! Firstly, the question will always make clear whether you are to consider ideas or style or both – so if it's style only and you write about ideas, then it's pretty obvious what your mark will be. Secondly, there will be some kind of context given to help you, i.e. not just 'Which writer's style did you find more effective?' but 'Which writer's style was more effective in making you think about abolishing exams?' Also, in the 2006 SQA exam, the question asked for a comparison of only certain parts of each passage, and, according to the Principal Assessor's report, many candidates didn't pay attention to this.

- Think of your answer to a comparison question as being like a little **essay**, with a structure, a clear line of thought, a couple of topic sentences, supporting evidence and linkage. It's a lot to ask for in the time available, but it's the only way to score good marks. Answers which are just a random jotting of ideas (no matter how many) get very low marks or none at all. It's worth remembering here that comparison answers are marked not on length but overall quality – good answers will score well, even if they're quite short.

- Leave yourself sufficient **time** if you want to have any hope of doing this question well. Anything less than 10 minutes is not going to give you much of a chance. On the other hand, it would be unwise to give it too much time at the expense of the other questions – you're never going to get more than five out of five.

- Consider having a quick look at the comparison question(s) **before you start**, so that while you are working your way through the other questions and becoming more familiar with the ideas and styles of the passages, you will be able to give some thought to what you might say in the comparison question(s).

DON'T

- Don't, when writing about style, just refer to and analyse small features of language in isolation. For example it could be that the brackets in line 1, the imagery in line 2, the repetition of 'no' in line 3, the minor sentence in line 4, the rhetorical question in line 5, etc. could all be referred to but only as a way of supporting a more general point about the writer's style. In comparison questions you should try to look at 'the big picture'.

- Don't fall into the trap of saying too much about one passage. You don't have to give the two passages equal treatment (that would be unfair, if you were arguing your preference for one over the other), but the question will always instruct you to refer to both passages.

- Don't write unconvincing and gushy praise disguised as evaluation: we've seen statements such as 'The writer's use of the semicolon in Passage 1 was fantastic' and 'The writer of this Passage uses brilliant words which help me to understand what he is saying'.

- Don't argue that you preferred one passage to the other because it was shorter (or longer) – it might be true, but it is not a valid point of comparison!

Competitive Sport

Read the following passages, in which the writers give their views about recent developments in competitive sport for young people.

The first passage is by Jackie Kemp, a journalist, and was published in *The Herald* newspaper. The second is by Gillian Bowditch, also a journalist, and was published in *The Scotsman* newspaper.

As you read, try to get a general grasp of:

- each writer's point of view about competitive sport
- the evidence she uses to support her point of view

and

- the style in which each is writing (pay particular attention to tone)
- examples of elements of the style.

Passage One

BRING BACK THE SPORTS DAY

Say 'school sports day' and memories come flooding back: the rough hessian sack tugged up to the oxters, feet straining at the seams as you waddled, hobbled or leapt across the field, the tie knotted tightly round two small ankles, the smell of hard-boiled egg, shell smashing as it fell off the spoon, the
5   excitement of inter-house or team rivalry, the strangeness of parents being there looking on, and the occasional (in my case, very occasional) delight of getting to wear a winners' ribbon. In 12 years at school, I have a vague memory of once making third in the wheelbarrow race.

As well as the silly races, there were athletics, children running full tilt, hearts
10   thudding in their chests as they pelted towards the finish line. Ancient trials of strength and skill, they were absorbing to watch and even those eliminated early on might sit and watch the contest unfold, tension rising as fewer and fewer were left in. One girl at my school was a beautiful runner, and I remember the thrill of watching her long legs eating up the track, sometimes
15   passing the others twice.

➤

Of course, some people have horrible memories of sports day, hating the feeling of being last, or under pressure to win from families taking it too seriously. Too much success made others over-competitive – witness Jeffrey Archer bringing spiked running shoes along for the fathers' race at his
20 children's school. But for most it was fun. One of the most abiding images of Princess Diana was of her running joyfully, shoes off and long neck extended, flying along the track in a mothers' event at her son's school, enjoying the simple pleasure of the race.

But the sports day has changed.

25 Almost a third of schools no longer have them at all, arguing that children without a chance of winning get nothing out of them. One school has barred parents, claiming their presence upsets the children. Others have replaced what they see as old-fashioned competitive races with a new concept: the 'zone sport day'. It is increasingly popular, but like many compromises it is a
30 poor, unhappy hodge-podge of a thing.

It does away with any individual competition and all obvious team competition, too. Children are sorted into *ad hoc* groups and go round a number of zones, doing a different activity at each one. For instance, they might run a relay but they will run it as a group, non-competitively. Their time
35 is recorded and then they go on to the next thing. At the very end, all of the times are added up and one group is declared to have won.

So instead of children running round a track, racing against each other while being cheered on by excited parents, they all shamble from zone to zone, not seeming to be particularly bothered about what's going on, or to be trying
40 hard, or to be emotionally involved in any way; in fact, many seem completely unaware of what is happening.

The scheme is supposed to have the advantage that all the children are active all of the time and therefore don't spend time watching each other, although cheering each other on and learning to appreciate the prowess of the natural
45 athletes among them were surely some of the more inclusive aspects of the traditional sports day.

I can testify that, for the onlooker, the zone sports day is perhaps the most tedious kind of sporting contest ever devised. I would rather watch paint drying. Devising a race so that there is no risk of losing, and no thrill of
50 winning, turns it into a dreary plod. More than tedious, it is depressing to watch the children doing something so pointless and boring. One wonders if

➤

it is a metaphor for the whole school experience, as they shuffle through exercises devised by higher authorities, which no-one has explained to them. They don't understand why it is being done this way and they haven't been
55 given a choice.

Surely it is time to resurrect the sports day and to bring back competitive sport. It is good for children and they enjoy it. Competition focuses the mind. We need not encourage them to take it too seriously and the 21st-century sports day is not going to recreate 19th-century social values, as some claim.
60 The sack race, after all, will go the way of the sacks. But for heaven's sake, let's get some perspective. Running races is OK. The race may not always be to the swift (although it usually is), but for the rest of us the life skill we learned at sports day of how to lose gracefully is something that will never be out of date.

Passage Two

LEARNING HOW TO LOSE

If you have any doubt about the intense and lasting psychological damage that can be wrought by competitive football, repeat after me: 'Scotland. World Cup. Argentina 1978.' In the pre-match sunshine of Buenos Aires, a reporter asked the Scottish manager, the late Ally McLeod, what he intended to do after the
5 World Cup. 'Retain it,' answered the ebullient McLeod, setting a benchmark for Scottish ineptitude which many have tried to equal but none has actually beaten. An entire generation's reserves of self-confidence were obliterated in one ill-starred adventure.

So, when a Council's 'football development officers' insist that losing a match
10 can have traumatic consequences, no Scot over the age of 25 is in a position to argue. Such mental scarring is bad enough for hardened football fans, who at least have alcohol and years of bitter experience to call upon. Just imagine what harm such trauma can wreak on young, impressionable minds.

Imagining is what we will soon have to do, however. Junior football teams in
15 some parts of Scotland are to be banned from playing in league and cup competitions in order to protect them from the pain of losing. In future, the losing side (henceforth to be known as 'the runners-up') will be allowed to field two extra players. If one team is more than five goals ahead at half-time, the score will revert to nil-nil.

➤

20   The rewriting of the Scottish rulebook echoes a row in England recently
when an under-nine junior league match in Sheffield ended 29–0, a score duly
reported in the local press. League officials have decreed that no scores above
14–0 can be made public and have asked the newspaper to refrain from
publishing them. The fear is that playing for teams which suffer such heavy
25   defeats humiliates children.

And they are right. But what the well-meaning officials fail to understand,
however, is that how to lose is one of the most valuable lessons of childhood.
The officials may believe that by eliminating the competitive element of
football, they are concentrating on teaching skills and social interaction, but
30   they are sending out a much more sinister message.

Children will learn that the rules can be rewritten to suit yourself, that
performance does not matter, that you need never push yourself to your
absolute limit and that losing must be avoided at all costs. In short, they will
learn that mediocrity is not merely acceptable, it is desirable.

35   Most children are intensely competitive. They can turn anything into a
contest: getting dressed, eating breakfast, breaking wind, behaving badly. You
name it; it is much better fun if you pit yourself against a deadly rival,
particularly if it happens to be a sibling. Attempting to eradicate competition
from a child's life is as pointless and cruel as trying to stifle their sense of
40   humour.

Sport teaches children to work together in teams to achieve a common goal.
It allows them to compete emotionally and physically in a controlled
environment. It provides an acceptable outlet for feelings of aggression
and it teaches them how to harness negative emotions and turn them into
45   something positive.

Any parent who has comforted a weeping child after a sporting disaster will
sympathise with what the Council officials are trying to achieve. But they will
also know that disappointment cannot be postponed indefinitely in life and
that it is easier to bear the more often it happens. If you never experience the
50   misery of losing, how can you experience the exhilaration of winning?

Questions

1.   Identify very briefly the key point of similarity in the writers' attitudes to
competitive sport.

2. To what extent do you agree with their point of view? Refer to the ideas/examples in the passages and to your own experience.

3. *(a)* Read lines 1–23 of Passage One.

Describe the writer's attitude to the traditional school sports day and show in detail how her choice of language helps to convey this. Refer closely to mood and tone and to how these are created.

(b) What function does line 24 perform in the passage as a whole?

(c) Read lines 25–55 of Passage One.

Describe the writer's attitude to the 'zone sport day' and show in detail how her choice of language helps to convey this.

(d) Read lines 56–64 of Passage One.

Describe the writer's tone in the concluding paragraph and explain in detail how her choice of language helps to convey this tone.

4. *(a)* Read lines 1–8 of Passage Two.

How effective do you find this paragraph as an introduction to the article as a whole? Refer to the style and ideas of the paragraph and to the ideas of the passage as a whole.

(b) Read lines 9–30 of Passage Two.

Referring to at least one example from each paragraph, show how the writer's language conveys her attitude to the people behind the changes she is describing.

(c) Read lines 31–50 of Passage Two.

(i) Describe in detail how the writer creates a predominantly impassioned and forceful tone in her concluding paragraphs.

(ii) Identify one point in these paragraphs where the writer's tone is very light-hearted and comment on the effectiveness of this sudden change.

5. Use your answers to the preceding questions (and any other points you think are relevant) to write a structured response to the following exam-type question:

Which writer do you think makes the more persuasive case in favour of competitive sport for young people? Justify your choice by referring to **the style of writing** in each passage.

Serving on a Jury

Read the following passages, which discuss the writers' experience of serving on a jury (in England it should be noted, hence the use of the word 'barrister', the English term for what in Scotland is called an 'advocate', i.e. the lawyer who presents cases to a jury).

The first passage is by Matthew Lewin, a writer and journalist, and was published in *The Independent* newspaper. The second is by Mark Steel, a newspaper columnist and comedian, and was published in the same newspaper eight days later.

As you read, try to get a general grasp of:

- each writer's point of view (i.e. is the jury system effective?)
- the evidence he uses to support his point of view

and

- the style each is using (pay particular attention to tone)
- examples of elements of the style.

Passage One

'Jury service? Don't worry, it will renew your faith in the jury system,' my friend assured me. But, two weeks and three trials later, I have emerged from a London crown court with my faith in our court system – and in my fellow jurors – severely battered.

5 For a start, as we gathered at 9a.m. on a foul and rainy Monday morning, there was a distinct shortage of the middle classes on display. Just about everyone with any means, commitments, high-profile or important jobs, and professionals such as doctors and dentists, architects and the like, seemed to have won deferment or exemption from the process. What was left was the
10 proverbial salt of the earth – just the sort of ordinary, sensible people that, you might think, you would want on your jury if you had been unjustly accused of a crime. The trouble was that they also included an inordinate number of people who did not speak English very well, and had serious trouble filling out the simplest forms and understanding the clearest
15 instructions.

> ➤

The vast majority had never seen the inside of a courtroom; nothing intrinsically wrong with that, I suppose, for why should they have if they had never been a witness or a defendant? The trouble was, however, that most of their knowledge and expectations seemed to have been acquired from
20   watching television's distorted concepts of courtroom procedure. Faced with the real thing, many jurors started drowning in the complexities.

Walking back to the Tube station one evening, I was accosted by a fellow juror, a young woman around 25 years old, who asked me: 'Are we supposed to be considering our verdicts tonight?'

25   'No,' I replied in amazement, 'we haven't heard the case for the defence yet.'

'What's that?' she asked.

The next day I watched her as the adversarial court system began to dawn finally on her consciousness with the defence case, the summings up by barristers and the judge's directions.

30   I was appalled at how many people on the three juries I sat on neglected to take notes - something that didn't stop most of them from 'remembering' volubly (but erroneously) in the jury room what witnesses, defendants, barristers and the judge had said in court. And, of course, they forgot huge tracts of evidence, no matter how crucial.

35   I was also shocked by how many of the jurors I sat with appeared to have no analytical ability whatsoever; no facility for ordering facts they heard, organising evidence in their minds or applying a kind of sequential logic to opinion - and decision-making - along the lines of 'If this is true ... then that must follow' and 'If we believe A then we can also believe B, and vice versa.'
40   Instead, jurors seemed to reach for facts and opinions in a totally random, haphazard way, seldom relating their views to any consistent approach to the body of evidence they had heard.

But what dismayed me most of all were the number of jurors who had clearly arrived with their own agendas - the main one being a deep distrust of any
45   form of authority and a thinly disguised antagonism to anyone in a police uniform. In all three juries there seemed to be a few hardliners who were on a mission to acquit, and refused to convict no matter how damning the evidence. (Most defendants in film and television courtroom dramas are innocent and fighting to clear their sullied names, so why should real life be
50   any different?) In two cases out of my three they prevailed to some degree,

➤

forcing the jury into majority verdicts and in one case forcing the jury to adopt a poor compromise that the judge later described as 'extremely generous' to the accused man.

55 Solutions? Well, I am not suggesting that juries be screened for intelligence, education or prejudice – a process that would run contrary to the concept of a jury being a random selection of one's peers. (And, in any case, who exactly would do the screening?) But, in the short term, something really has to be done to reduce the incidence of able, well educated people avoiding jury service and thereby distorting the mix of abilities on the jury panels.

60 And I am convinced that there needs to be better training for jurors – better than the brief and partially inaudible video presentation that we saw on the morning we arrived. There has to be a proper induction process, possibly on the Friday before jury service begins, which should include a visit to a courtroom and a thorough explanation – perhaps with a bit of role playing by 65 jurors – of court processes and the kind of thinking that should be applied.

Everyone remembers the classic film, *Twelve Angry Men*, in which a lone juror, played by Henry Fonda, bravely holds on to his convictions and, in the process, saves an innocent man from being convicted. The film I would make would be called *Twelve Stupid Citizens*, and would show deeply ignorant 70 people acquitting obviously guilty criminals.

Passage Two

I've been fascinated by the letters to *The Independent* discussing jury experiences in light of Matthew Lewin's recent article. Best of all was the reader who complained that the whole system was flawed because his co-jurors spent all day trying to complete a crossword. Can this be entirely 5 accurate? Surely even a judge would notice if, halfway through a witness's evidence, the jury was squabbling over whether the Seine or the Rhine was the one that went through Germany. Maybe the judge thought that, as it was the last day of the trial, the jury should be allowed to bring in games.

What seemed to annoy the letter-writer most was that although it was called 10 a 'coffee-break crossword', it took them all day to finish it, thus proving we're entrusting justice to idiots. Perhaps, instead of being able to replace individual jurors before a trial, a defendant should be able to make an entire jury do a

➢

'fastest-on-the-buzzer' test, like on Who Wants To Be A Millionaire. Then your verdict is decided by the one who puts four famous buildings in the right

15   order of height in 4.6 seconds.

I was once on jury service, and felt certain my co-jurors would vote to convict the timid teenage Nigerian defendant, as two police officers had witnessed him selling dope, and he had several chunks in his pocket, which he'd claimed was for his personal use. But the officers contradicted themselves over several

20   details, and one officer said he'd heard the defendant talk to a Spanish couple in Italian, except for the one English sentence, 'I want to sell you some hash'.

At that point, I wondered how to calculate exactly how many errors, logically, linguistically and philosophically, were contained in that one piece of evidence, especially as neither of the other officers mentioned this incident at

25   all. Nonetheless, I felt bad for the multilingual dope boy, especially when I saw the juror on my left, a stern woman with the face of a Victorian headmistress – a hanger and flogger for sure. We were sent off to consider our verdict, with the judge's advice: 'You must use your own life experience.'

As soon as we arrived in our little room, I saw that every juror had taken their

30   responsibility incredibly seriously. Everyone had taken notes, listened intensely throughout, and was eager to clarify areas of confusion.

I suggested the police evidence was flawed, and gave a couple of examples. Then a woman bus driver gave better examples, and a nurse did the same. So the advertising executive asked if anyone at all believed the police evidence,

35   and the Victorian headmistress said brusquely: 'As far as I'm concerned, the police were telling a pack of lies.' One by one, everybody agreed, so the foreman said: 'Well there's no point in discussing that part of the case at all then.' Then the advertising executive methodically laid out the rest of the case. I wondered whether he was going to come up with a nifty slogan, like:

40   'The evidence mounts that he's not sold an ounce.'

The one issue remaining was why he had several chunks of dope, having apparently spent all his money. 'Well,' said an architect, 'it's no more strange than someone going to France for two months' worth of wine. He was just stocking up.' A teenage girl said: 'I've sometimes blown all my wages in one go

45   on a pair of shoes. He's just done it with dope.' And an endearing Jamaican pensioner said: 'I've seen men in the music business smoke that much in one afternoon. There, the judge told me to use my life experience, so that's what I've done.'

➢

That is part of the beauty of the jury system. A judge has a life experience
50 entirely alien to that of most people who are tried. Just as obvious is that
when people are given a chance to make decisions that have a real impact,
they almost all respond with inspiring enthusiasm. In a jury, your voice
genuinely counts, your decision has an impact and it will be acted upon, so
it's almost the opposite of a vote in a general election. Which is why, in a jury,
55 no one ever says: 'Oh, I can't be bothered to vote. Guilty, not guilty, it doesn't
make any difference; all those verdicts are as bad as each other.'

It took us 45 minutes to find the lad not guilty – unanimously. As we all left
the court, the nurse, whose name I never knew, said: 'I think we did a good
thing today,' and I skipped to the underground station, exhilarated by the
60 humanity of these 11 strangers.

Questions

1. Identify very briefly the key difference of opinion about the jury system.

2. Note other significant points of disagreement (for example, about the experience
    of serving on a jury, opinions about fellow jurors, etc.).

3. Identify, with examples, key features of each writer's style, paying particular
    attention to tone.

4. Use your answers to the preceding questions (and any other points you think are
    relevant) to write a structured response to the following exam-type question:

    Which writer do you find more effective in making you aware of important issues
    about jury service? Justify your choice by referring to **the ideas and style** in each
    passage.

The Importance of Reading

Read the following passages, which were written by well-known writers of children's fiction. The first passage is by Michael Morpurgo (author of more than fifty books, including *Why the Whales Came* and *Kensuke's Kingdom*) and was printed in *The Times* newspaper. The second passage is by Anthony Horowitz, author of the 'Alex Rider, teenage spy' books. It is part of a public lecture he gave in 2005, which was reprinted in *The Telegraph* newspaper.

Passage One

ONCE UPON A TIME WE READ OUR CHILDREN STORIES

For the past 18 months in my role as Children's Laureate I have been travelling the country telling stories to young readers and young writers, telling how this particular weaver of tales writes his stories. Like some superannuated strolling player, I have set up and performed wherever anyone
5   would let me: in tiny village halls, grand concert halls, in tents and bookshops and school halls and, once, in an old people's home; from audiences of 14 children in the small island school on Jura, to 2,500 people in the Albert Hall.

Hundreds of my fellow writers, and storytellers, illustrators, librarians and booksellers do the same. This kind of sustained effort to bring children to
10 books and books to children is much needed and is, in my view, the most effective way of persuading children to become readers and writers. Here is someone in front of them who loves stories, who tells them with such passion that the world of reading, the sheer joy, fun and wonder of it, can be opened up to children who may never have enjoyed books at all. A young life can be
15 changed that way, enriched for ever.

Yet why do we fail to engage so many children? Why do millions of them never become readers? After all this commitment, why is there this divide in our society: books beloved by some and ignored and regarded as irrelevant by others? Why are stories not central to our culture, unless they are on
20 television? Why do so many feel alienated from their literary heritage?

➤

The convenient answer is the usual answer. Blame someone. Parents, teachers, librarians, publishers, bookshops, the media or the Government. The uncomfortable truth, I have concluded, after years as a father, teacher, writer and, now, as strolling player, is that we are all responsible because we are not

25 being honest about this. Parents who do not read to their children enough at night, teachers who use books simply as educational tools for the 'literacy hour', librarians who allow their libraries to become drab, publishers who publish too much rubbish (there are 10,000 children's titles a year) and writers - for we are complicit in this overproduction - are all responsible.

30 However, the question should not be 'Who is to blame?' but 'What can be done about it?' What practical steps can be taken to make reading and writing more inclusive and attractive for our children? If we want our children to be literate, to love stories, then bring storytelling back into the mainstream media. We had Listen with Mother on the radio, we had Jackanory on the TV.

35 Where are they now? Bring parents in on the act - that is how reading should begin, almost with the mother's milk, that intimate story between parent and child.

Yet we know it will often be through the teacher that a child first hears a story. Many great teachers find the time to read stories and to read them well,

40 so that children will hear the music in the words, and will laugh and cry with the teacher. Thus the teacher passes on his or her own love of stories to their children, talks of books and writing and reading with confidence, fervour and delight. Teach the children a love of story, of the music of words first, give them the delight, inspire them to write themselves, then the need for literacy

45 begins to make sense - literature before literacy, then.

How can this be done? Unchain the teachers, take the fear of targets away, unlock their creative potential, give them back their freedom to teach what it is they love. Trust them. Let there be half an hour at the end of school simply for telling and reading stories, a wonderful wind-down at the end of each day.

50 But don't ask questions afterwards, just let the children listen and enjoy, and lose themselves in the magic of it.

We need to exercise our children's imaginative powers through reading and writing. For what is education if it is not to broaden our horizons, give us knowledge, understanding and insight and the opportunity to empathise and

55 learn about ourselves and the complex world around us. I know no better way for a child, or a grown-up child, to do this than through books.

Passage Two

THOU SHALT READ

Children and reading seems to be a hot topic. Do boys read? Are they reading less than girls? These are questions that are being asked more and more often – and recently the Government climbed on the bandwagon. But who cares? Does it really matter who's reading what – and, at a time when increasing
5 numbers of children's books are being launched with ever larger fanfares, what is it that we are all chasing? Culture, literacy, civilisation and enlightenment? Or film deals and six-figure advances?

The Government has announced a £27 million initiative to distribute nine million books to children aged up to the age of four. 'Every child deserves the
10 best start in life,' it proclaims. 'And there is no better time to get parents into the habit of reading with their children than when they are little.' It is embracing the work of Booktrust, an independent educational charity founded in the 19th century, which has, indeed, managed to place millions of books into the hands of infants and children.

15 I admire the work of Booktrust, but I was surprised that nobody showed the least concern about this new alliance. Because it seems to me that, at a stroke, the agenda has changed. We have moved from pure altruism – the sharing of an enthusiasm – to the simplistic attitude of another governmental tick list. Reading is good for you. We're giving kids books. So the Government is good
20 for you.

Consider the dangers. If politicians and their advisers become involved in this project, who will end up choosing the books? And how long will it be before certain rules – of political correctness and good citizenship – set in? Once the Government is involved, what will happen to publishers who entertain
25 writers like me? Would my own publisher be happy for me to be critical of the Government if, at the same time, it was negotiating a contract for several million copies of Maisie Mouse? Perhaps I'm being paranoid but I think we should be wary of lines getting crossed.

What I most dislike about the Government's take on literacy is this 'nanny
30 state' feeling that reading is good for you. I just hate the idea that if you read, you're going to be all right; that books can act like vitamins or diet supplements to make a healthier, happier human being.

I love books. I love reading. I can't imagine my life without it. But I do resent the idea of reading being some sort of virtue, a sort of gold medal that you can

➤

35 pin on the lapel of some pink-faced, grinning child. I hate parents who tell me that their little Gemma is only nine but already she's halfway through *War and Peace*. It all seems so Victorian – and it's hypocritical, too.

Are adults reading? And what are they reading? And how bad does a book have to be before it's not worth reading at all? Step forward Jeffrey Archer, perhaps.
40 Does reading *Hello!* magazine count as reading? How about Mills & Boon? Where do you draw the line between literature and (not to put too fine a point on it) crap? When does reading become good for you?

People like Dan Brown's books, although I think his writing is terrible, with its clichés, its melodramatic bombast and its clumsy constructions. Well, it's
45 easy enough to sneer at Dan Brown, but however critical you want to be, you have to admit that his stories – and in particular, of course, *The Da Vinci Code* – are wonderfully readable. That's what's made him even richer than J. K. Rowling. His books sell in millions. Whether they have any inherent value is actually irrelevant. And that is precisely my point. Reading is enjoyable. I can't
50 imagine my life without books. All my work has been informed by my love of Dickens, Hardy, Austen, Orwell and so on. I like Stephen King, too. And Ian Fleming.

But reading is not necessarily a quick fix, and we delude ourselves if we think that it is. The boy who reads is not necessarily better than the boy who
55 doesn't. Did Beethoven read? Did Mozart? Does Bill Gates or Richard Branson? I sometimes think we're trying to turn reading into a universal panacea. It's many things – but it certainly isn't that.

Questions

1. Identify briefly the key similarity and the key difference in the writers' attitude to reading books.

2. To what extent do you think the title of each passage provides an effective introduction to the ideas of the passage?

3. Which passage do you find more effective in stimulating your thoughts about the importance of reading? You should refer to the **ideas and/or style** of both passages. (Indicate clearly at the start whether you are referring to ideas or style or to both.)

'Public Grief'

Read the following passages, in which the writers give their views about the way some deaths are mourned in public.

The first passage is by Katie Grant, a columnist with *The Scotsman* newspaper. It was written in October 2004 after the death of Mr Kenneth Bigley, an engineer from Liverpool, who had been taken hostage in Iraq and subsequently killed by his captors. These events were given extensive coverage in the media.

In the second passage, Peter Preston, a former editor of *The Guardian* newspaper, looks at the public and media reaction to the death, in November 2005, of the Northern Ireland footballer George Best.

As you read, you might find it useful to note down key points in the development of each writer's argument, and important features of style in each passage.

Passage One

THE CHEAPENING OF GRIEF

In my church yesterday morning, we prayed for the murdered hostage Kenneth Bigley after we had prayed for a faithful parishioner who died in his bed. I breathed a sigh of relief, not because I downplay Mr Bigley's suffering and appalling death, but because it restored some kind of counter to the
5 extraordinary coverage his story has received. When the priest, quietly and simply, using no flowery phrases or specially portentous voice, asked us to remember Mr Bigley and his family in our prayers, I felt, for almost the first time since he was seized, able to do so without cringing or feeling manipulated. My prayers may be useless, but at least I felt that what I was
10 expressing was both genuine and appropriate and that at last I was not being obliged to listen while somebody who never met Mr Bigley attempted to turn a perfectly ordinary person into a paragon of innocent virtue and altruism, with no accolade too strong and no praise too unstinting.

I wonder, though, how many other people in Britain were allowed to do the
15 same. If the death of Mr Bigley has illustrated anything at all, it is that many British people, particularly those involved in the media, have become incapable of dealing with anything involving suffering and death with

$\geqslant$

sympathetic but cool heads. Ever since the Princess of Wales died in 1997, whenever something untoward happens, we are first prompted, then almost 20 obliged, to rush about emoting publicly, signing books of condolence, buying flowers, lighting candles and being willingly coerced into silences of varying lengths – all for people we never met. How you grieve for those figures who find themselves selected by the media for special attention, is no longer a personal matter. Grief has become manipulated, municipalised or even 25 nationalised. Had you been in Mr Bigley's home town of Liverpool yesterday and quietly carried on your business during the two minutes of silence, preferring to deal with his death in your own way, you would have found yourself frowned on at the very least, and frowned on with those special, self-righteous frowns people use to indicate that you are being thoroughly 30 disrespectful and have not a feeling bone in your body.

I find such coerced grief invidious and false. In this particular case, when media pundits are sent to Liverpool to observe 'the city's grief', it becomes almost surreal. The overblown, 'whole city in mourning' rhetoric, while appropriate for something like the Hillsborough football stadium disaster, has 35 almost made a mockery of the very real and poignant tragedy of the death of one man. It is too strong to say that Mr Bigley's life has been hijacked a second time, but we are not far off it. Mr Bigley may, for example, have been very fond of Iraq and its people, but, although you can forgive his family for saying so, he was not actually there for altruistic purposes. He was there to earn a great 40 deal of money on which he intended to retire.

And why not? There is nothing shameful in that at all. It becomes shameful only when a perfectly honest and decent truth, which does not belittle Mr Bigley in the slightest, is deliberately submerged under a syrupy veneer of fake sainthood designed expressly to make us feel that his death was even more 45 tragic than it is already. Indeed, far from squeezing yet more sympathy out of the collective British heart, the attempted canonisation of Mr Bigley has ensured that much sympathy has been tainted with cynicism.

Grief is an extremely important human emotion and I do not belittle it. I understand, too, that the barbaric nature of Mr Bigley's murder has made a 50 certain ghoulishness inevitable. But when sentimental or ghoulish tears flow too easily, we cheapen grief, just as we do when we turn a dead man's life into a sugary confection. Mr Bigley was not a hero. He was an ordinary man who went to a country to earn money in the full knowledge that it was very dangerous and paid the ultimate price. It is not a glamorous truth, but it is the 55 truth and although it has been a terrible thing, if you don't want to cry about it, you should not feel you have to.

Passage Two

WHY THIS PARADE OF GRIEF?

Now that the fever has abated a little, it is possible to tackle the question muttered dozens of times over the past few days. Why this parade of grief over George Best? What does it mean? The answer – the infernally complex answer – is also simple at heart. We weren't doing it for him; we were doing it for us.
5 We were treating ourselves to a 'Diana moment'.

The original Diana moment came in 1997 when we saw the vast crowds lining the funeral route to Westminster Abbey and heard the swell of dissent as they took sides: for her, against Charles and his unfeeling family. It seemed utterly spontaneous. It caught the royals and their advisers flat-
10 footed.

Joe Public was standing up to be counted, to have his demonstration of distress and resentment watched around the globe. Why should pomp and circumstance come controlled, purveyed only by reverent-voiced BBC commentators, when the people's princess was savagely lost? Joe Public
15 helped make 15 minutes of famous history that he would always remember – and could tell his grandchildren about. He wasn't anonymous any longer, a speck of humanity brushed away by the rich and powerful.

The death rituals of Diana were a surprise. Nobody – especially not the media – had foreseen what would happen when you mixed a cocktail of tabloid
20 romance, majestic melodrama and genuine tragedy. Nobody was prepared for the moment that followed. But how quickly we learn.

Would the Queen Mother have her moment too? As commentators measured her age against Diana's youth, it seemed not. Perhaps Joe Public would sit this one out? But no: there at last was the moment, a queue of condolences
25 winding miles along the Thames. It was another brief encounter with history, another ad hoc definition of vague, swilling concepts such as nationhood and community.

And so the pace quickens. Pope John Paul II – iconic, controversial, loved – draws unprecedented throngs to St Peter's Square when he dies. Rome has
30 never seen scenes to equal this, a city taken over by millions of mourners – and thousands of TV cameras. This is history, isn't it? Twenty four-hour cable news churns on.

➤

Where, among such arc-lit sessions of sorrow and so much digitised despair, do balance and reality lie? That particular question has no answer as yet. There
35 is no reason why ordinary citizens of our increasingly instant, wired world shouldn't be allowed to weep alongside their leaders and peers, to bring their own circumstance to traditional pomp. But we're getting ever closer to the edge.

Now, George Best sets a benchmark along the funeral route. Let's be clear. He
40 was, for a few years, one of the most charismatic footballers around. There are a few terrific TV clips of goals he scored 35 years ago. Middle-aged football commentators relive their youth when they talk of him. The nostalgia of the beautiful game comes drenched in tinted memories. His death is certainly cause for pause, lament and reflection. But to see the Diana moment turned
45 into the George moment is to see the media hearse rolling heedlessly downhill.

There is nothing strictly logical about the magic that transformed a washed-up footballer into a surrogate Princess of Wales. But there is something calculated, almost cynical, to the process. The media, surprised by
50 the Diana moment, don't want to be surprised again. If Sky News keeps a vigil outside the hospital where Best is dying, then BBC News 24 must be there as well. Call for the obituary writers and football sages and video libraries. Kill a few more forests. Order a million black arm bands and minutes of silence in stadiums around the land. Give Joe Public another chance of 'being there', of
55 being part of something he and his kids can remember – like a bit part in a reality TV show.

Questions

1.   Identify very briefly the key point on which the two writers agree.

2.   Read Passage One again.

   (a) Explain why Katie Grant 'breathed a sigh of relief' (line 3) in church, and go on to summarise the main points in her argument.

   (b) Show in detail how she makes clear her distaste for what she calls 'coerced grief' (line 31). You should examine especially lines 14–47 and consider such features as word choice, sentence structure and tone.

3. Read Passage Two again.

    (a) According to Preston, who is more responsible for the 'Parade of Grief' – the public or the media? Justify your choice by close reference to the passage.

    (b) Preston's tone is often quite cynical. Give some examples of this and explain how each example makes the cynicism clear.

4. Use appropriate material from your answers to the preceding questions (and any other points you think are relevant) to write a structured response to **one** of the following exam-type questions:

    (a) Which passage gives you a clearer picture of the influence of the media in manipulating 'public grief'? Justify your choice by referring to the **ideas** of both passages.

    (b) Which writer's style do you find more effective in conveying her/his attitude to 'public grief'? Justify your choice by referring to the **style** of both passages.

Terrible Teenagers?

In this Set, there are three passages, all discussing the attitude of the older generation to teenagers.

The first passage, written in May 2002, is by Jackie Kemp, a columnist with *The Herald* newspaper; the second, written in August 2005, is by Jenny McCartney, who writes for *The Telegraph* newspaper; and the third, written for *The Times* newspaper in May 2004, is by Kate Figes, a writer whose books include *Life After Birth* and *The Terrible Teens*.

You should read all three passages. At the end you will be asked to make your own choice of two passages to compare – and you can decide whether you want to write about ideas or style (but not both).

Passage One

LET'S MAKE THE YOUNG LEAD THE WAY

Do we need obedient children? No. What we need in the 21st century is creative, questioning, challenging children who can think for themselves. We no longer need to prepare them for a life of kowtowing to the old bowler hat, the gaffer, the policeman, the dominie, the sergeant-major. That world is gone
5 for ever. Belief in unquestioning obedience began to subside as the world assessed the aftermath of the Somme and the Holocaust, and it will never come back.

We need to produce young people who are immensely flexible, self-sufficient, full of cheek and confidence. We need to leave behind the put down and the
10 threat in the same way that we have put away the belt and the cane. We need to learn to listen as well as to teach, to cherish the bright spark and not to seek to put it out.

We do need children to co-operate, to come to school, to participate in society. But if they are not co-operating we need to ask them why and
15 negotiate to fix it. We need to encourage them to solve their own problems and find solutions they can live with. With truancy, perhaps we should face the fact that school isn't right for everyone; many children suffer from school

➣

phobia because of bullying or unhappiness. We need to look at answers such as counselling or small learning units.

20 Surely all this is obvious. Yet the Government in England has gone down the Dickensian path of supporting the jailing of a mother whose children failed to attend school, and the tenor of the public response is that this has been demonstrably a Good Thing, that it has 'worked'.

No – it is a disaster.

25 There are parents up and down the country struggling to impose rules and regulations on recalcitrant teenagers and failing. It is well documented that the parents of many badly-behaved children far from being from bohemian, kaftan-wearing luvvies are, actually, already strict, heavy-handed disciplinarians who are trying in the only way they know – with threats, fists and
30 ill-controlled anger – to make their children conform. Pushing these parents into a corner by subjecting them in turn to threats and fear from the state is only going to make these relationships break down faster. In many of these families, the currency of discipline and punishment is already so devalued that another step on the road will bring them to the end of it and we will have
35 runaways as well as truants.

Thank goodness for devolution. Jailing truants' mums is not going to happen north of the border, but just in time to stop us getting smug, it was revealed recently that researchers have found in focus groups across the country that most Scots think of young people as 'a problem, a nuisance, and a threat', and
40 that their hard-line demands include a curfew on young people and harsher sentences for youth crime.

Some of that is indicative of social attitudes towards children as much as it is the problems they have and cause. The young have few real friends outside their own families these days. They are more and more seen as their parents'
45 'problem'. Yet the older generation should ask themselves who is going to push their wheelchairs and take care of them in old age, who is going to run the country, who is going to have the ideas that generate economic success for Scotland in the future.

After all, the children are our future. We need more than ever now to find ways
50 to encourage their creativity and confidence so that we can produce home-grown talent that can compete on the global stage. We need them to have ideas and the courage to put them into practice, to have the strength to risk failing.

➤

55 Britons like to mock the education system in the United States with its reliance on Big Bird and new ideas such as using rap in English lessons, whereas countries such as Japan with lots of homework, rote learning, blackboards and exams are seen as more successful educationally. But look at how the US has developed computer and IT technology. Most of the important technological innovation of the past 10 years has come from people who

60 came through the US school system, in large part because they are encouraged to think for themselves and a high value is placed on creativity.

In Scotland, we need to empower young people through freedom, choice, and co-operation. Make them strong and let them lead the way.

Passage Two

PUT THE FEAR OF GOD INTO THESE THUGS

A miserable state of affairs has come to pass at St James's church, near Rochdale. A malevolent gang of local teenagers has been intimidating elderly worshippers, forcing the Rev Robin Usher to hold weekday services in his home instead. The teenagers have taken to loafing around the church grounds

5 and the graveyard, smoking dope and swigging alcopops. Sometimes they chuck stones and eggs at the church windows, or thunder up and down one wing of the church while the elderly folk cower in the other, struggling to keep their fraying thoughts on God.

The plight of the parishioners is by no means unusual: they are the hapless

10 victims of The Rampaging Teenager, a burgeoning social phenomenon. Not so long ago The Teenager was a relatively benign figure, subject to jovial censure largely for sulkiness and a penchant for loud music. Now The Teenager is a national terror, filling older people with a queasy unease.

Every day The Teenager makes an unlovely appearance in the press,

15 sometimes in the form of an individual who has perpetrated an especially shocking act, but more often as part of an uncontrollable mob, dissolving teachers' authority in jeering obscenities, terrorising bus drivers, wielding knives and mugging Tube passengers.

It is true, of course, that the thousands of exemplary adolescents hardly

20 ever make the papers, apart from at exam results time when they are briefly

➢

emblazoned across the news pages, the gleam of their teeth competing with the high sheen of their results.

Yet even taking the press's preoccupation with wickedness into account, it seems indisputable that the minority of 'problem teenagers' – as once they 25 would have been called – are becoming ever more violently problematic, just as adults are becoming ever more wary of confronting them. These two things are quite certainly connected.

When I am travelling on the top deck of the bus, for example, and gallumphing 15-year-olds are shrieking oaths, dropping litter, guzzling 30 pungent kebabs and pushing one another about, do I stand up and demand that they sit down and behave like normal people? Of course I don't. I am worried that, by attempting any such gesture, I might be baited mercilessly until I can finally stumble off at my stop. I have little confidence that any other adult on the bus would back me up. Teenagers now are awful, I think.

35 But then, every so often, I have little flashbacks into my own unbalanced, excitable teenage psyche. I was reasonably respectful towards grown-ups, but – seen through adult eyes – my state of mind was far from normal. Several times a day, some minor idiosyncrasy I had observed in my teachers – people whom I broadly liked and respected – would trigger in me prolonged fits of helpless, 40 tearful laughter. Almost everything seemed intensely funny, and few of us had any profound sense of consequences. I remember my English teacher, pale-faced, brandishing a large lead weight which he said had come hurtling down the stairwell, narrowly missing his head. The culprit was a quiet, quirky boy who had been rolling his interesting lead weight along the top of the 45 stairwell when it tumbled off. It could have killed our teacher, but at the time we simply thought the incident a diverting little hoo-hah in a dull afternoon.

Yet such incidents were admittedly rare, and what contained their frequency – and prevented mere silliness from escalating into systematic taunting and aggression – was a sense of a unified adult authority, whereby parents, 50 teachers, policemen and everyone else appeared to think as one, and were virtually certain to back each other up. That authority has been gradually eroded and fragmented by a tremulous, legalistic officialdom.

Teenagers do not quite understand, although they should, that a hurled egg might seem a great joke to them – and a source of sheer terror to an elderly 55 lady; but aside from a few very hard cases, they are more reckless than wicked. It is up to adults to assert their vanished authority over the lunatic adolescent fringe. That is why the congregation of St James's church should spurn prayers in the vicarage next week, and – with a couple of towering policemen to hand – prepare to retake the church and its grounds.

Passage Three

IN PRAISE OF THE LOWLY TEENAGER

Teenagers seem to make headlines only when it is bad news – binge-drinking, truancy, drug-taking, underage sex. No other age group is so consistently stereotyped, misunderstood or reviled. The public views them with suspicion – pedestrians will cross the street rather than pass three or four noisy
5 teenagers on a street corner – while to anyone working behind the counter, every teenager is a potential shoplifter. Meanwhile, parents complain endlessly about them: their untidy rooms, their selfishness, their back-chatting, the difficulty learning where they've been, what they've been doing and with whom.

10 So maybe it's unusual to say that I love teenagers. I love having my 15-year-old daughter's friends in the house. I buy extra tubs of ice-cream just to keep them there, despite the extra clearing up. I love hearing them shriek happily. I love the way that six of them can cuddle up on a two-seater sofa discussing world poverty, eating popcorn in front of an episode of *Friends*.

15 Adolescents exist in a half world, often denied both the security of childhood and the privileges and responsibilities of adulthood, with no obvious rites of passage, no clear path from one to the other. They're considered adult when it suits, but not when it doesn't; they have to pay adult prices and tax, but they still can't vote.

20 Last week it was revealed that the Government does, in fact, intend to give the vote to 16-year-olds after the next election – welcome news indeed, for it is high time that we began to harness the passionate political energy of the young. Our political life feels so tired and short of ideas and solutions that it can only improve by involving them more.

25 We think of teenagers as materialistic, which they often are, yet this is also a time when they are at their most altruistic, idealistic and determined to make the world a better place. They begin to grasp the significance of more abstract concepts such as religion, relationships and mortality. They wake up to the wider world and feel outraged by its injustices. That anybody should be
30 homeless when there are empty houses seems ludicrous. Wars are a crime against humanity – end of story.

Teenagers embrace concepts such as vegetarianism because of their need to do something when they feel angry about animal welfare. They can argue for hours about political ideas and be caring and public-spirited provided they

➤

35 are given opportunities and encouraged to do so. Their arguments are often simplistic and categoric, for they have yet to develop a deeper understanding of how hard it is to find solutions to the world's major problems. But their idealism is fresh and forthright, passionate to the point where it can challenge the old fogeys.

40 We criticise adolescents for being rebellious and rejecting authority, but maybe they are just being honest, an attribute that we lose the moment we need to please a boss. Teenagers have the energy and the daring to challenge bureaucracy and pointless rules. 'You can't wear two pairs of earrings at school but you can wear one. But if you can wear one, why not two?'

45 Teenagers may be morose and monosyllabic at times, but they can also be hilarious. They love to exercise their expanding intellectual skills playing with irony and puns. And where would we be without the vibrancy of youth culture, without the pop anthems? Our language is kept alive with new definitions of words such as 'cool', 'fit' or 'safe'.

50 Teenagers are acutely sensitive and vulnerable. They often mask a deep sense of self-doubt with bravado. Negative images of teenagers do not do them any favours, for such stereotypes reinforce negative images about themselves when they feel down. If we tell them that they are selfish, lazy, good-for-nothings, they just rise to those expectations: we create the
55 impression that that is how you have to behave to be a teenager today.

But if we look for the positive we find in the young a well full of potential. Teenagers may seem like threatening outsiders, but that is because we fail as a society to integrate them as valuable constituents. They will behave in a more mature manner only when they are afforded respect and more adult
60 responsibilities. Giving 16-year-olds the vote is one significant step, for it tells them that their views matter and includes them in the political process from which many feel alienated.

Questions

Choose any two of the passages and answer **either** of the following questions:

(a) Which passage do you think more effectively conveys the writer's views about the relationship between adults and teenagers? Justify your choice by detailed reference to the **style of writing** in each passage.

or

(b) Which writer's view of the way teenagers are (and should be) perceived by adults are you more inclined to agree with? Justify your choice by detailed reference to the **ideas** of both passages.

Part Three

Close Reading Practice Papers

Part Three

Introduction

There are six full-length exercises, based closely on the model of past Higher English papers. The number of words in each exercise is broadly similar. In most cases the first passage is longer than the second, but in Paper Three the reverse is the case. The order of the passages is dictated by the material and its accessibility to students, following the general principle that the second passage should benefit from an informed reading of the first.

The content and style of each passage dictate also the proportion of questions devoted to understanding and analysis: one passage may offer mostly understanding questions to guide the student through the ideas involved, while the other may be ripe for analysis and evaluation of techniques related to description, persuasion, entertainment or indoctrination.

The particular combination of passages in any exercise also has an impact on the section of the paper where questions on both passages are asked. The important point of comparison between the two passages may be related to the different ideas on the same topic, or may be in the different presentation of the same ideas, or in different points of view. As a result a comparison question (or questions) could ask for a comparative evaluation of stylistic techniques, or of the strength of the 'argument' or of the cogency of the ideas related to each passage, or, indeed, a combination of these. The work in Part Two will have prepared students for these possibilities.

It is difficult to gauge the comparative difficulty of these six exercises, but the choice of order has been predicated on the idea that the first two or three are on subjects fairly familiar to young adults and therefore might provide a comfortable starting point. However, no attempt has been made to provide 'transition' exercises between the level of demand at Intermediate 2 and Higher: these are all full-blown Higher exercises. There is a minimum level of competence which has to be reached before any benefit can be gained from tackling them. The work in Part One is designed to help with building the necessary knowledge and skills. These exercises can be used for early diagnostic assessment but their best potential is probably to be realised in the second half of the course when the students are sufficiently skilled to make a meaningful attempt at tackling a full-scale exam exercise.

Teen Magazines

Passage One

In the first passage journalist Jenny McCarthy responds to recent criticism of a pre-teenage girls' magazine and goes on to discuss its contents.

DROOLING OVER BOYS

The publishers of *Mad About Boys* – a candidly-titled magazine aimed at nine to 12-year-old girls – must have been weeping into their spreadsheets last week. First, Dr Michele Elliott, the director of the children's charity Kidscape, accused them of making up the 'sweet little girl' on the cover 'to look like a
5 French tart'. That might have been regarded as helpful publicity, had not Woolworths promptly announced that it was banning the magazine and called upon other retailers to do the same.

I can see, on first glance at the magazine, exactly what Dr Elliott means. 'Look Delish For Your First Date' the cover-line promises, and beside it smirks a
10 strangely knowing, lipsticked child with piled-up hair and a neck-choker. She is holding a frame containing a photograph of one of the numerous boys she is allegedly mad about.

The French Tart look hints of garret rooms, and hectic nights in Montmartre, and sloe-eyed hussies stumbling from the pages of a nineteenth century
15 French novel. As a perennial fashion stand-by, the French Tart is up there with the Young Sophisticate (Audrey Hepburn in *Breakfast at Tiffany's*), or the Screen Vamp (Marlene Dietrich in *The Blue Angel*). All of these 'looks', however, carry the frisson of sexual self-consciousness, and that is why they are so disturbing when worn by a pre-teenager.

20 Yet the truth is that little girls – however grossly unpalatable it might be to adult tastes – love nothing more than caking themselves in unsuitable make-up, and tramping around in outsized high-heeled shoes.

I can remember, as a rather plain, skinny child, being wistfully obsessed with the trappings of femininity. I recently saw a picture of myself aged ten, with a
25 body like a pipecleaner; my face was free of make-up, but – in a flailing, aspirational gesture – I had painstakingly painted my toenails scarlet. Shortly

➤

afterwards, I persuaded my aunt to accompany me to a department store to get my ears pierced. My chief aim, as I recall, was to prevent people from mistaking me for a crop-haired boy. A week later, wearing my new earrings, I
30 went for a walk with my father. We met a genial acquaintance of his, who took one look at me and boomed, 'And what age is your son?'

My happiest moment was when, for my 11th birthday, my brother bought me a black eye-pencil. But the difference between then and now was that the retail industry had not latched on to the galloping spending power of
35 the pre-teenage 'Tweenies'; we were dependent on the occasional indulgence of our elders. Today, the shops offer nine-year-olds all the glittering tat their avaricious little hearts desire, at prices they can afford: frosted nail polishes, 50p earrings, lacy hairbands and mini-lipsticks in a thousand nasty shades.

The French Tart phenomenon might be disquieting, but I do not think that
40 it is the main drawback to *Mad About Boys* and magazines of that ilk. Little girls will always want to practise looking like adult women – if we dressed like Mary Poppins and carried outsize handbags, so would they, but we don't. The chief problem with *Mad About Boys* is there in its title: its craven, relentless obsession with the opposite sex. Its readers, presumably,
45 go for the older man: hence the endless pictures of grinning, 15-year-old 'sexy lads to pin up on your bedroom wall'. The fashion pages ask: 'Ever wondered what gear lads find really sexy?' The quiz is: 'Who's your ideal guy?' At the age of 10, oddly enough, most little girls haven't attempted to work that out. When the *Mad About Boys* reader gets a bit older, she might
50 move on to *Mizz* magazine ('Do chat-up lines really work?' and 'What boys talk about when you're not there') and then to *Sugar* ('Will that boy become a boyf?' and 'Win his heart right now'). By the time she reaches the age of consent at 16, she will already have been mad about boys for an exhausting seven years.

55 One wonders, when the *Mad About Boys* reader finally grows up, where all the mania for boys – drummed into her from an early age – will actually go. The madness is not for one boy in particular, note, but for 'boys' as a general concept, boys as a form of devouring hobby. Will she be mad about boyfriends, mad about her husband, and then mad about all her husband's
60 friends? Will she be mad about adulterous liaisons in hotel-rooms in the afternoon? Or is there a moment at which the erstwhile *Mad About Boys* reader is supposed to set aside a lifetime of assiduously-practised 'flirting skills' and sexy 'chat-up lines' and say: 'Forget that. Now I'm really mad about sailing single-handed round the world'?

➤

65   It is a strange paradox: when the majority of women were economically
dependent on men, little girls' magazines were full of articles on books, or
ponies, or ballet dancing, or how to knock together a handy cupboard for the
bedroom. Now that most women have jobs and salaries of their own, they are
about nothing more than drooling over boys.

Passage Two

In the second passage sociologist Imelda Whelehan wonders, in her book Overloaded:
Popular Culture and the Future of Feminism, *if teenage girls' magazines show any
evidence of the 'Girl Power' phenomenon of the 1990s.*

SUGAR AND SPICE?

'Girl power' of the type proclaimed by the Spice Girls, with its rhetoric of
choice, control and empowerment, most certainly caused some kind of quake
among pre- to early teen girls in the latter half of the nineties, but it is difficult
to gauge its real impact, since contemporary media trend-watchers are always
5   too happy to construct a fanfare around a small ripple. Until these young
women enter the world of work or higher education it is difficult to know
whether it will have any lasting effect. At the moment its visible effects are the
most obvious ones and they seem in sum to offer a reassertion of traditional
models of femininity, with younger and younger girls showing more of their
10   prepubescent flesh decorated by fake tattoos.

Teen magazines, criticised in recent years for their sexual explicitness,
perhaps offer evidence of how girl power has filtered into the teen
consciousness, yet from the ones I have studied there are no images of
empowerment. To take three examples, *Mizz* is aimed at pre- to early teens,
15   *Sugar* at teens, and *Minx* late teens. None devote much space to aspects of
young women's life not associated with boys and looking good, how to fill in the
time between dating boys with make-up and beauty tips, celebrities and soaps.

Health education in one issue of *Mizz* was limited to 'eight things you didn't
know about smoking', and advice to a 'worried Michael Owen fan', who
20   thought she might become pregnant through heavy petting, to 'take your time
and don't feel pressurised into doing anything you aren't ready for'. In many
ways *Minx* does read like the logical extension to *Mizz* – its total elision of
the world of work suggests its pure teen focus, with only a greater emphasis
on celebrity interviews, soaps, beauty, fashion and the addition of sex, travel
25   and health. *Sugar*, which claims to be Britain's best-selling girls' magazine, has

➤

a younger readership and relationships with boys tend to be described rather disingenuously in terms of 'snogging'. Sexual matters only really feature in the problem page, or by extension in its features, such as the one about a 17-year-old who had her baby at home ('I almost gave birth in a loo!').

30 Even though there are token references to female friendship, the magazines, just like the *Jackie* of my generation, emphasise fashion, beauty and boys. Fear of being different and non-conformity are constant laments in the pages that deal with embarrassing moments. These magazines offer little support to the ideals of self-determination and autonomy, setting much greater store on
35 fitting within society's ideal. If anything, attitudes to boys are less healthy, if that could be possible, than when I was young, and life is generally described as one long scramble to get a 'lush lad'. Both titles, *Minx* and *Mizz*, promise an irreverence and feistiness which they never deliver – and like the title *Sugar* implies, they are all syrupy and rather unwholesome.

40 In my reading of girls' magazines I would have to agree with that doyenne of feminism Germaine Greer, who declares that 'the British girls' press trumpets the triumph of misogyny and the hopelessness of the cause of female pride'. All girls' magazines seem to do is prepare children for the world of glossy women's magazines which will open up further vistas of anxiety about one's
45 body, one's boyfriend, one's lifestyle, one's attitude. It would be conceptually naïve not to understand that magazines, dependent as they are on advertising revenue, need to trade on a sense of lack; but it also explains why they never extend beyond the 'girl power' model of feminism. No wonder young girls' lack of self-esteem or ambition is reaching epidemic proportions.

Questions on Passage One

1. Read lines 1–19.

    (a) What does the writer mean when she says the publishers of *Mad About Boys* were 'weeping into their spreadsheets'? **1 U**

    (b) Explain briefly what, according to lines 1–7, brought this about. **1 U**

    (c) Why, according to lines 8–19, is the writer inclined to agree with Dr Elliott's criticism? **2 U**

    (d) How does the writer's word choice in lines 8–19 emphasise her disapproval of the magazine? **2 A**

2. Read lines 20–38.

   (a) In what way do lines 20–22 act as a turning point in the writer's line of thought?   **2   U**

   (b) Referring closely to the language of lines 23–26, show how the writer pokes fun at herself.   **2   A**

   (c) How effective do you find the anecdote in lines 27–31 in illustrating the writer's point in this paragraph?   **2   E**

   (d) Show how the writer's attitude to today's 'retail industry' is made clear by her language in lines 32–38. Refer in your answer to more than one language feature.   **4   A**

3. *(a)* Explain in your own words what, according lines 39–54, the writer sees as the 'chief problem' about *Mad About Boys*.   **2   U**

   (b) Show how the writer's language creates a humorous tone in lines 44 ('Its readers…')–54.   **2   A**

4. Read lines 55–64.

   (a) Explain in your own words two problems the writer predicts for readers of *Mad About Boys* when they grow up.   **2   U**

   (b) Show how the writer uses sentence structure in these lines to highlight the problems.   **2   A**

5. *(a)* Explain in your own words the 'paradox' to which the writer refers in line 65.   **2   U**

   (b) How effective do you find the last paragraph (lines 65–69) as a conclusion to the passage as a whole? Refer in your answer to the ideas and/or language of the paragraph.   **3   E**

   (29)

Questions on Passage Two

6. *(a)* What, according to the opening sentence, did 'Girl Power' seem to offer?   **1   U**

   (b) Why, according to the writer in the rest of the first paragraph, is it 'difficult to gauge its real impact'? (lines 3–4)   **2   U**

7. *(a)* How does the context of lines 11–17 help you to understand the expression 'no images of empowerment'? (lines 13–14)   **2   U**

    (b) Referring closely to the language of lines 18–29, show how the writer makes clear her contempt for the magazines she describes.   **4 A**

8. Read lines 30–39.

Explain in your own words the writer's key criticism of the way the magazines deal with:

    (a) girls' place in society;   **2 U**

    (b) girls' attitudes to boys.   **1 U**

9. Consider the last paragraph of the passage (lines 40–49).

    (a) What, in your opinion, is the tone of this paragraph?   **1 A**

    (b) Explain in detail how this tone is created.   **3 A**

                               (16)

Question on both Passages

10. Which passage, in your opinion, more effectively explores the shortcomings of teenage girls' magazines?

Justify your choice by referring closely to the **style of writing** of both passages.   **5 A/E**

                                (5)

                 Total marks   **(50)**

[END OF QUESTION PAPER]

Paper Two

Fight to Save Our Food

Passage One

Colin Tudge argues that modern food and farming policies cause much avoidable harm, driven as they are by the twin motives of profit and the availability of cheap food.

THE FIGHT TO SAVE OUR FOOD

Modern food policies are screwing up the world. In all countries - but of course, particularly in poor ones - they are killing people, in a variety of ways. They are overriding traditional cooking with all its family and social customs. They are destroying rural economies and the life that goes with them. For
5　good measure, modern farming is gratuitously cruel to animals and, despite occasional ad-hoc legislation, it is getting worse.

Yet we are supposed to accept and admire the scientists, tycoons, and politicians who are bringing about the changes because, they claim, the despoliation that we see all around us represents 'progress'.

10　There's already a lot of protest. But if humanity really cares about humanity we need to grasp the nettle - to acknowledge that the present generation of 'experts' and leaders have got it all horribly wrong. We (meaning all of us) have got to re-think agriculture from first principles - ask what it is, and what we really want from it, and how to get the world back on course.

15　Do I exaggerate? Not at all. The bedrock point is that it's technically straight-forward to feed all the people in the world well, with food that's abundant, nutritious, and safe. But that's not how things are turning out. Famines are still common (almost routine in Africa) while 800 million people worldwide are currently undernourished. Yet in more and more countries, from the Americas
20　to the Far East, hunger now persists side by side with gross obesity. A common sight in modern Beijing is two trim parents brought up in harsher days with an unfortunate, ponderous globe of a child. These are the fruits of the modern food industry we are all supposed to believe is working selflessly on our behalf.

25　Another major point is that most scientific 'progress' in agriculture is developed by Western corporations. These developments are not designed to

➤

tackle the real problems of local farmers but to make profits for their creators. The reality of farming at the moment is that common sense has been sacrificed for profit.

30 And the three ingredients of profit, as any businessperson knows, are as follows.

The first is to maximise production. So modern farming is as productive as possible – even when the country is producing vast surpluses, as is the case in Europe and the US. The second is to minimise the cost of production, which
35 means cutting labour. Britain and the US now employ little more than 1% of their workforce on the land – in the US there are more people in prison than there are full-time farmers. People are replaced by big machines and by industrial chemistry. The third ingredient is to 'add value'. British governments, in particular, like to claim that cheap production leads to cheap
40 food, but this is another con. A survey by the Real Meat Company in the west of England recently showed that their own sausages cost only half as much as the cheapest brands in the supermarket. The Real Meat sausages look much dearer – £3.50 per pound against £1.75. But they contain four times as much lean meat. Supermarket shoppers pay for filler.

45 Globalisation is making the whole caboodle worse. Every farmer in the world is now engaged in a global dogfight with every other farmer. First-world farmers cut costs by cutting labour and mechanising. Some third-world farmers throw their lot in with Western corporations (farming is the modern imperialism) or else work for slave wages. Meanwhile Western supermarkets
50 make a virtue of buying at the lowest possible price – which means from the world's most desperate farmers.

It's a gloomy picture. But it's one that we can fix. For it is possible to feed people well, and to look after the environment, and to support agrarian economies, and to be kind to livestock – but only if we design an agriculture
55 expressly for that purpose. What we need is an 'enlightened' agriculture, rooted in sound biology – the biology of human beings, of plants and animals, and of the world as a whole. Just as farmers work out how much food to give a chicken or pig, so we must think about how much food human beings need. Then we need to see how the world itself can physically provide what's
60 needed.

That's the theory. In practice, enlightened agriculture reflects nature. The most suitable land should be used for the most important crops, the staples like cereals, pulses and potatoes. The richest land is for fruit and vegetables.

➢

65 Yet this isn't a vegetarian formula. There is plenty of room for the traditional rearing of livestock. But we must play to the strengths of the different kinds of animals. Cattle and sheep are ruminants – great at eating grass, which grows on hills and wet meadows where cereals cannot be grown. Traditionally, pigs and poultry were kept to eat leftovers and this should remain their role. In addition to keeping fewer livestock, all farms should be as mixed as possible.

70 But present day farming, in the hands of global corporations and at the service of massive supermarkets, is organised quite differently. In the pursuit of profit, it aims to maximize meat production. Half the world's wheat, three quarters of the maize and an incredible 90% of the soya is grown for livestock. Animals raised on such a vast scale become our competitors.

75 In physical terms, at least, enlightened agriculture is easy, little more than common sense. But as governments and supermarkets have abandoned common sense, in the meantime, we will have to take matters into our own hands.

What are the ways of doing this? Well, a surprising number of farmers are still
80 trying to practise good husbandry. Consumers should try to seek them out. Organic farmers can be a bit more anti-technology than seems sensible but they too are carrying the flag of good husbandry, and deserve support.

In the short term we might pay more for good food that's well raised. But in the longer term the prices will come down if there is a demand and
85 producers supply more. Also, governments and supermarkets might discover the error of their present ways and come back into line. The game's not over yet – but if sanity doesn't prevail it soon will be.

Passage Two

Hugh Fearnley-Whittingstall wonders whether in the light of the news that fast food outlets are closing he could look forward to further changes in the nation's eating and shopping habits.

I'M LOVIN' IT

We all have our fantasy headlines – the announcement of events of global or national significance that chime irresistibly with our own personal values and ambitions. Well, I got to see one of mine this week: 'Fast food giant to close 25 stores in the UK'. Yes! For me, and no doubt others who share my loathing of

➤

5 giant global corporations, this is an air-punching moment. All morning after I heard, I was wandering about in daze of delighted disbelief. And when I'd done with the air-punching, I went for the double forearm salute, shouting 'YES!' again, through clenched teeth, to my two clenched fists. A childish reaction, perhaps, but schadenfreude is primordial stuff. And the bigger the
10 beast that's fallen, the greater the glee. In short, I'm lovin' it!

It is not that fast-food culture is on the wane – far from it. In fact, the takeaway sector generally continues to grow. But as it expands, it is also diversifying. These days, in the clusters of fast-food outlets in our major cities, we are starting to find, dotted among the big names in burgers, chicken and pizza,
15 some genuine alternatives: the big-name coffee shops, of course, but also juice bars, sushi restaurants, fruit and nut stands, bagel bars, pasty parlours, soup and salad takeaways – and even the occasional organic burger joint. Taking the fast-food sector as a whole, the possibility of an encounter with what we might call 'real food' is definitely on the up.

20 This is particularly encouraging, not because of any significant change in the sense of where we are now, as much as where we might get to in the not-too-distant future. In the newest, most innovative forays into fast-food there is an emphasis not only on healthy alternatives, but transparency, traceability and the provenance of ingredients.

25 For me, the biggest boost to come from this week's welcome headline is the sense it gives of what changes might now be possible elsewhere in the food sector. It gives heart to other campaigns that strive to liberate our food culture from even more powerful corporate beasts.

The real stranglehold on our food culture, comes not only from the behemoth
30 fast-food brands, but from the big supermarkets. Between them, they control 75% of the grocery market in the UK. There are hundreds of thousands of farmers and food producers, here and all over the world, selling groceries to tens of millions of British shoppers. Yet the growing, processing, distribution and sale of all that food is controlled by these organizations. That has to be
35 unhealthy.

For me, then, the true tipping point will come when significant numbers of consumers begin to say to the supermarkets: enough of your screwing down of prices to farmers and producers; enough of your misleading labelling and spurious nutritional information; enough of the systematic suffering of livestock
40 in intensive systems; enough of your dirty, polluting, wasteful food miles.

➤

The way to be effective is to change the way you shop. You don't have to stop going to supermarkets, but you do have to take from their shelves only those products you believe are honestly and ethically traded, transparently labelled, environmentally sustainable, and not abusive of either animals or people. And

45 go elsewhere for the rest.

Then I might just get to see one of my other fantasy headlines: 'Shoppers desert supermarkets for born-again high streets'.

Questions on Passage One

1. 'Modern food policies are screwing up the world.' (line 1)

What are the consequences of modern food policies, according to the writer? You should answer in your own words. **3 U**

2. Show how the writer's tone in lines 7–9 is made clear by the language he uses. **2 A**

3. Read lines 10–29.

   (a) What are the two major points the writer makes in lines 15–29 about how the 'leaders have got it all horribly wrong'? (line 12) **2 U**

   (b) How do sentence structure **and** word choice in lines 10–29 persuade the reader to adopt his point of view? **4 A**

4. Read lines 30–44.

   (a) Comment on the impact and function of lines 30–31 in the development of his argument. **2 A**

   (b) Explain what, according to the writer, is the disadvantage of each of the 'ingredients of profit'. **3 U**

5. Read lines 45–51.

   (a) Explain why globalisation makes the situation worse. **2 U**

   (b) How does the writer's word choice in these lines accentuate the idea that globalisation is detrimental to farming? **2 A**

6. Read lines 52–60.

   (a) Briefly state the writer's solution to the problems identified in the previous paragraph.   **1**   **U**

   (b) Show how sentence structure in these lines helps to support his argument.   **2**   **A**

7. '…enlightened agriculture reflects nature.' (line 61)

   Using your own words as far as possible, give any **three** examples of this which are described in lines 61–69.   **3**   **U**

8. Show how the word choice **or** tone of lines 70–74 emphasises the writer's criticism of present day farming.   **2**   **A**

9. Read lines 75–87.

   What course of action does the writer recommend in these lines and what does he hope might be a consequence of this action?   **2**   **U**

       (30)

Questions on Passage Two

10. Read lines 1–10.

    (a) In your own words explain the writer's definition of a fantasy headline. (lines 1–3)   **2**   **U**

    (b) Show how the language of lines 3–10 highlights his appreciation of the fantasy headline mentioned in lines 3–4. You should consider more than one technique in your answer.   **4**   **A**

11. How does sentence structure in lines 11–24 emphasise the variety and quality of the takeaway sector?   **2**   **A**

12. Read lines 25–35.

    Why is the sentence 'The real stranglehold…big supermarkets' (lines 29–30) important in the structure of the argument of the passage?   **2**   **U**

13. Read lines 36–45.

    In what ways do the writer's structure **and** punctuation clarify his attitude to supermarkets?   **4**   **A**

14. How appropriate is the final paragraph (lines 46–47) in the
context of the whole passage?   1   E

                                                                    (15)

Question on both Passages

15. Read lines 30–87 of Passage One and lines 25–47 of Passage Two.

Which writer is more effective in giving you an idea of the power
exercised by supermarkets and the chances of that power being
diminished by the public?

Justify your choice by referring to the **ideas and style** of both passages.
You may wish to consider such stylistic aspects as structure, word
choice, tone, imagery...   5   E

                                                                    (5)

                                                Total marks   **(50)**

[END OF QUESTION PAPER]

The Generation Gap

Passage One

In the first passage journalist Melanie Reid welcomes the findings of a survey into the attitudes and lifestyles of young adults.

'WEIRDNESS DUST' NO MORE

Time was, if you were 18, in possession of sound mind and enough motor function to transfer food into your mouth, there was unquestionably something wrong with you if you were still living at home. Living with your parents was a crushing label of failure and only very sad young people did so.

5 Those were the days, so accurately defined by Ruby Wax in her autobiography, when you felt your parents were sprinkled with 'weirdness dust'; and you didn't risk staying around to get coated, too.

Time was. Time is, and nearly a quarter of young Britons in their twenties are still living with their parents, the majority of them extremely happily. To the

10 amazement of anyone born prior to 1970, staying with your mother and father is now socially acceptable, even chic. This new trend is called 'lifelong parenting', and many of today's children hold an open return ticket back to the parental home.

Today it's perfectly cool to be in your twenties and still living with mum and dad.

15 There is no other conclusion to come to, when 54% of young adults said they were happy to be at home and did not want to move out. A significant proportion had returned home three times or more, after flying the nest, and were content to stay. Even when children do leave, it seems to be on exceptionally good terms: two-thirds of young adults up to the age of 30 admit they continue to

20 receive money from their parents even after they have left home.

In a world beset with social-trends surveys which are almost invariably gloomy – mental ill-health, cancer rates, pensions, divorce, school standards; you name it, things are getting worse – this is one of the sunniest things I've read in months. Quite simply, we are getting kinder to each other. The findings

25 indicate how much more love, respect, and tolerance there is in circulation than there used to be. This is a clear sign that contained within the bedrock of human life, the family unit, there is warmth and affection and social cohesion.

➤

Of course, there is still bad parenting. But away from the extremes of deprivation, abuse, and drug addiction, the majority of today's parents are far
30 better at bringing up children than their parents were. Far, far better. There is a whole generation at present in their fifties and sixties who had fathers who went through the Second World War. Many of these men were hard, damaged, remote disciplinarians, inches deep in weirdness dust. Many were incapable of expressing emotion. They were rotten fathers and – to put it mildly – difficult
35 to live with: their children escaped the family home as soon as they could.

Those refugees are today's parents: the generation who, in many cases, rebelled against the coldness and the discipline and convention of their own childhoods; who were determined to break the cycle. Their children grew up being shown love and affection; they were granted freedom. Home, therefore,
40 is a place to head for, not to escape. It is that subsequent generation which is now hanging on at the hearth, relishing the memories of happy childhoods and spending time with their mother and father for enjoyment, not just out of duty or necessity. They are the ones, in effect, who are building the concept of family for future generations.

45 Modern family life is not disintegrating, it is merely changing. Modern life is contradictory, supple, unstructured; nothing lasts for long and old boundaries have disappeared. Different generations have never needed each other more. Lifelong parenting is nothing less than today's young people deserve, for their energy and courage is wonderful.

Passage Two

In the second passage Deborah Orr provides a similarly enthusiastic response to the survey's findings.

THE WAR OF THE GENERATIONS MAY SOON BE OVER

It seems that people are beginning to see having children as a long-term commitment, extending deep into adulthood. Far from longing for the day when their kids are 'off their hands', parents now are in for the long haul. This new trend has been christened 'lifelong parenting', and is predicated on the
5 findings of a new survey which reveals that while one in four Britons in their 20s is still living with their parents, more than half of these young adults don't actually want to move out at all. Living as an adult in the parental home, until recently seen as the pathetic compromise of the socially stunted, is once again reasonable.

➤

10 I'm not sure whether this really constitutes 'lifelong parenting' – although the term is designed also to encompass statistics that among people in their 20s who have left home, two thirds rely on their parents for some form of financial help. But I do think that in these times of unrelenting bad news about the fragmenting family, this vision of the consolidating family is

15 something to be celebrated. For while such banal difficulties as 'the cost of living' are obviously contributing to the trend, these facts also, surely, give rise to the hope that the toxic trench so many families in recent decades have found themselves sliding into is finally being filled in.

For decades we have been obliged to normalise, in that cute but

20 uncompromising phrase 'the generation gap', a painful process whereby parents find their children are living in a world with entirely different rules and morals to the one they were brought into. The result, in the fairly recent past, has sometimes been parents and children who are irreparably alienated, or at least able to reach only the most fragile of compromises about the shape

25 of each other's lives.

These clashes, even though they have been characterised merely as the battle of age against youth, have actually been much more deep-rooted than that. In a time of unprecedented change in social, sexual, cultural and consumer attitudes, it is within families, among parents and children, that individuals

30 have been called to personal account for seismic shifts in acceptable behaviour across society as a whole.

In 1952, for example, when my parents were teenagers, cohabitation accounted for 2 per cent of first partnerships among young adults. Now, half a century on, that figure is 75 per cent. Many parents now confronted with a child who

35 wishes to cohabit will recognise such an arrangement as one they themselves found to be both flexible and beneficial. In fact, if they don't much like the partner in question, they may count the limited commitment as a blessing.

But when my parents found out that I was living with my boyfriend, they were devastated. Trying to explain to them that such a relationship was neither

40 unusual nor damaging was quite impossible. They judged by the standards of their own youth, and were quite convinced that I was so much under his evil influence that I was dangerously deluded. At the time, my parents seemed to me to be the dangerously deluded ones, living in the dark ages and determined that I, their only daughter, should have to hunker down there with them.

45 Now I see what a terrible situation they were in. I was, after all, still a teenager, and a particularly difficult one at that. Crammed with daft ideas and an

➤

unshakeable belief in my own invulnerability, I made a dozen idiotic choices
and lunatic decisions every week. Why on earth should my parents have been
able to set aside those aspects of their wayward daughter, and put this latest
50 act of capriciousness down to a changing world as much as a 'rebellious
child'?

The truth was that we were caught in a moment in time – the early eighties
– when the 'generation gap' was wider than it had been at any point in history.
The possibility of living my life in a way that resembled the life I wanted,
55 while under my parents' roof, did not exist. How could we share the same
home, when we didn't even live in the same society? For young people now,
a couple of generations into the massive social liberalisation we have
experienced since the Second World War, the situation is not so extreme.

To an extent, the generation gap is still very much with us, but nevertheless
60 the gap in social experience that left parents and their children living in
entirely different cultures is thankfully closing fast. So while conservative
critics tend to think of social liberalisation as a never-ending process, destined
forever to weaken social cohesion and endlessly to marginalise the family, the
truth instead may be that what we have been through is merely a scary and
65 difficult period of adjustment, but one to which an end is very much in sight.

For half a century now, the generation gap has been vast, a clash of values so
profound that it seemed to many to represent not just a gap but a chasm. Yet
maybe, as the new sexual landscape settles down, and the generations are able
to set down the cudgels, the sheer good sense of a commitment to 'lifelong
70 parenting' will help people to recognise the obvious fact that you can't just
make a baby with any old person, then expect, not much later on, to be able
to write them out of your life.

Questions on Passage One

1. Read lines 1–20.

    (a) According to the writer, what change has taken place in young
    people's attitude to staying at home? Answer briefly and in
    your own words. 1 U

    (b) Show how aspects of the writer's sentence structure highlight
    the idea of change. 2 A

(c) 'Today it's perfectly cool to be in your twenties and still living with mum and dad.' (line 14)

How appropriate do you find the language of this sentence in the context of the writer's argument? **2 A/E**

2. Read lines 21–27.

    (a) Explain in your own words why the writer is so pleased at the results of the survey. **2 U**

    (b) Show how the writer's imagery in the final sentence of the paragraph reinforces her point of view. **2 A**

3. Referring to lines 28–44, explain in your own words as far as possible the key differences the writer claims there are between parents now and parents from the previous generation. **4 U**

4. Why, according to the writer in the lines 45–49, have different generations 'never needed each other more'? **2 U**

(15)

Questions on Passage Two

5. Read lines 1–18.

    (a) Explain in your own words what used to be society's attitude to young people who continued to stay in the parental home. **2 U**

    (b) To what extent does the writer feel the term 'lifelong parenting' is an appropriate one? **2 U/E**

    (c) How effective do you find the writer's use of imagery in lines 13 ('But I do...')–18 in conveying her point of view? **4 A/E**

6. According to the writer in lines 19–25:

    (a) What does the term 'generation gap' mean? **1 U**

    (b) What are its effects? **2 U**

7. Read lines 26–37.

    (a) How effective do you find the writer's word choice in lines 26–27 in conveying her point of view about the generation gap? **2 A/E**

    (b) Explain how the context of lines 32–37 makes clear the meaning of the expression 'seismic shifts' (line 30). **2 U**

   (c)   How effective do you find the last sentence of lines 32–37 as a conclusion to the paragraph?   **2** **E**

8.   Read lines 38–51.

   (a)   Show how the writer's language in lines 38–44 conveys the strength of her parents' reaction to her living with her boyfriend.   **2** **A**

   (b)   Show how the writer's language in lines 45–51 conveys her awareness of her own foolishness.   **2** **A**

9.   Read lines 52–65.

   (a)   What does the expression 'social liberalisation' (line 57) mean?   **2** **U**

   (b)   Explain in your own words as far as possible what critics of 'social liberalisation' believe is wrong with it.   **2** **U**

   (c)   What does the writer believe may be the truth about it?   **1** **U**

10. To what extent do you find the ideas and language of the final paragraph (lines 66–72) appropriate as a conclusion to the passage as a whole?   **4** **E**

                                                      (30)

Question on both Passages

11. Both writers approve of the change in attitudes revealed by the survey. Which one more successfully engaged your interest in her point of view?

      Justify your choice by referring closely to the **style of writing** of both passages.   **5** **A/E**

                                                      (5)

                                   Total marks   **(50)**

[END OF QUESTION PAPER]

Watch Your Words

Passage One

Political language may seem like waffle, but in fact it uses carefully chosen phrases in a bid to persuade us by stealth. In the following passage Barry Didcock takes us on a journey through political language from George Orwell's 'Newspeak' to its modern cousin 'Unspeak'.

TAKING POLITICIANS AT THEIR WORDS

As George Orwell knew – and Winston Smith, his most famous literary creation, found out – language can be every bit as useful a weapon as bombs and bullets. In the novel *Nineteen Eighty-Four* the lethal lexicon is Newspeak, defined in modern dictionaries as 'a propagandistic language
5   marked by euphemism, circumlocution, and the inversion of customary meanings', and itself a fictional version of a language Orwell first wrote about in his celebrated 1946 essay, *Politics and The English Language*. 'Political language has to consist largely of euphemism, question-begging and sheer cloudy vagueness,' Orwell wrote. 'Defenceless villages are bombarded
10   from the air, the inhabitants driven out into the countryside, the cattle machine-gunned, the huts set on fire with incendiary bullets: this is called pacification.' If our own 21st century politicians had read that before they opened their mouths, they might have thought better of uttering such phrases as 'war on terror'.

15   Or would they? For some keen political watchers, these circuitous phrases are not like the clumsy euphemisms of old but are instead prime examples of Newspeak's even more virulent and duplicitous 21st century offspring – Unspeak, 'a mode of speech that persuades by stealth'.

The definition comes courtesy of journalist and author Steven Poole who is to
20   rhetorical doublespeak what the small boy was to the naked emperor: a pin to prick the speech bubbles. He has written a book, *Unspeak*™, which sets out the case against, and also offers a forensic analysis of, some of the most notorious examples he has found.

Poole, who has read Orwell, describes his experience the first time he heard
25   the words, 'war on terror'.

➤

He thought it was quite a bizarre phrase, and on looking around he saw that the same sort of rhetoric was operating in all areas. He realised it was a special kind of deceptive language that politicians used in many areas of discussion. It is commonly thought that what politicians say is just hot air or waffle, but
30   in fact, although they are trying to deceive us with the language they use, they can't help but betray what their hidden motivations are.

One of his favourite examples is 'climate change', the term preferred by the governments of the US and Saudi Arabia when discussing global warming. Intensive lobbying by them in the late 1980s saw the phrase 'global warming'
35   replaced in official UN terminology by 'climate change'. The reason? 'Climate change' sounds less frightening; can refer to cooling down as well as heating up.

It is a classic piece of Unspeak and its genesis and use proves that Unspeak is now viewed as a vital cog in the machinery of government. Carefully tooled
40   phrases conveying an entrenched political position while appearing to do no such thing are scattered like seed to the wind. And it works: by reframing the debate about global warming through the use of Unspeak, progress towards a genuine solution has slowed, which benefited those whose interests lay in oil and gas.

45   But what happens when competing Unspeaks lock horns? The abortion debate is the best example of this. The pro-abortionists were the first to discover Unspeak, rallying under the label 'pro-choice' in the 1970s. But they were later gazumped by the anti-abortionists, who plumped for the even better sounding 'pro-life'. Nobody would be anti-life, would they?

50   Now the good news. All Unspeak terms have a shelf life. The phrase 'concentration camp' was first used by the British to describe the prison camps in which Afrikaners were interned during the Boer War. But what was a neutral term in 1900 became unusable after 1945 when the scale of the Nazi genocide made the phrase anathema to future generations.

55   Similarly, we are now starting to see behind the smoke and mirrors – or should that be exhaust fumes and windscreens? – of 'climate change'.

Unspeak can work temporarily and then it loses its persuasive power. People realise what it means. That is the kind of process that we can try to accelerate if we stand up to these phrases wherever we see them. The Unspeak victory
60   of climate change is running out. But it was a very good delaying tactic for about a decade.

➤

So what can we do to fight the growth of Unspeak? Simply pay attention. Complain when phrases such as 'war on terror' are used unquestioningly by the media, look behind phrases such as 'climate change' and 'pro-life' and try
65 to see what's really hiding in the murk.

George Orwell finished his essay on politics and the English language with a similar exhortation. 'One cannot change this all in a moment,' he wrote, 'but one can at least change one's own habits, and from time to time one can even, if one jeers loudly enough, send some worn-out and useless phrase . . . into the
70 dustbin, where it belongs.'

Orwell proposed 'melting pot', 'acid test' and 'veritable inferno', all examples of what he called 'verbal refuse'. Half a century on, political discourse is still plagued by those phrases, but that shouldn't stop us adding a few to Orwell's list. So, allow me to propose a few 21st century candidates: 'collateral damage',
75 'smart bomb' and 'surgical strike' are three to be starting with.

Better still, let's see them off with 'repetitive administration of legitimate force' - that's 'beating to death' in Unspeak.

Passage Two

In this passage Rafael Behr also considers Unspeak, but he feels that Poole's attack on political jargon goes too far.

WEASEL WORDS AND FORKED TONGUES

When military commanders draw up their plans, they assume they will be going into battle against armies. They do not usually factor in the threat from abstract nouns. Politicians, on the other hand, know better, which is how we ended up fighting a 'war on terror'. To the soldier, this is ridiculous. 'Terror'
5 cannot sign treaties. It cannot surrender. But that is what makes it so attractive to the politician. The language of war is used to smuggle all sorts of extreme measures - detention without trial, torture, military aggression abroad - into what is really a time of peace.

This is 'Unspeak', a word that Steven Poole has coined to describe those terms
10 that have crept into our everyday language with political spin built in. 'War on terror' is an American import, but we have homegrown Unspeak too. 'Antisocial behaviour' is a good one. Everybody seems to know what it is without it ever having been defined. We know, for example, that hooded

➤

15 youths loitering in an apparently intimidating fashion on poorly lit street
corners is 'antisocial behaviour'. But, as Poole points out, when young people
congregate like this, they are, in fact, exhibiting very social behaviour, only in
a manner that is perceived as creating discomfiture. They are not breaking the
law or, at least, not until they are subject to an ASBO (which defines their
behaviour as criminally antisocial). Then, if they continue to act 'antisocially',

20 they can be imprisoned. It is normally dictatorships and theocracies, not
democracies, that legislate so intrusively on what a society deems good public
conduct.

Anti-democratic habits ooze out wherever Poole breaks the crust of political
jargon. The great 20th-century dictators knew as well as modern political spin

25 doctors that the expression of truth depends on language. Control the words
and you control the truth. Orwell knew this too. 'Unspeak' is the modern
cousin of Big Brother's Newspeak in *Nineteen Eighty-Four*.

Journalists, in particular, risk pushing a partisan agenda by carelessly importing
the terms that politicians would prefer they use: 'extraordinary rendition'

30 instead of 'kidnap and torture', for example. Poole charts the stealthy
legitimisation of 'ethnic cleansing', which started out as a term liked by the
perpetrators of genocide because it hid their crimes in a metaphor of hygiene.
By dropping the inverted commas, we adopted the murderers' point of view.

It is certainly possible for horrible truth to be stronger than euphemism. A

35 'purge' used to be positive – the expulsion of something poisonous –
therefore a good thing. That is why Stalin borrowed the image to describe his
massacre of party members to make it appear to be positive. But in this case
the enormity of the crime changed the word, rather than the word softening
the impact of the crime. No one would announce a management shake-up or

40 a corporate downshift or a cabinet reshuffle these days by saying they plan to
have a 'purge' – the word now has too many violent connotations.

Poole's archaeology of everyday terms is impressive and salutary, but it is too
pessimistic. Not every metaphor is meant to trick. He cites politicians' overuse
of the word 'tragedy' as a sign that they want bad events to be seen as acts of

45 God, not their incompetence. But it is more likely politicians just abuse the
word in much the same way that football commentators misuse it when they
describe a team's 'tragic' exit from the cup. No less irritating, but not sinister.

There is no doubt that Unspeak is among us and that we must guard against
it. But we should also allow ourselves a little faith that the truth shines

50 through in the end.

Questions on Passage One

1.   Read lines 1–14.

    (a) In your own words give two factors which 'Newspeak' in the
          novel *Nineteen Eighty-Four* and 'political language' as defined
          by Orwell in his 1946 essay seem to have in common.   **2 U**

    (b) By referring to particular words or phrases, show how the
          example in lines 9–12 ('Defenceless… pacification') illustrates
          one of these factors.   **2 A**

2.   Read lines 15–23.

    (a) Show how the word choice in lines 15–18 reveals the concerns
          of 'keen political watchers'.   **2 A**

    (b) Show in detail how the comparison in lines 19–21 suggests that
          the writer regards Steven Poole as an effective campaigner against
          the political misuse of language.   **2 A**

3.   What does the sentence 'It is commonly thought…' (lines 29–31)
    tell us about politicians' language?   **2 U**

4.   Read lines 32–44.

    (a) Explain fully why the term 'global warming' was changed to
          'climate change' and what effect this change had.   **3 U**

    (b) Show how imagery **and** sentence structure in these lines assist
          in emphasising the writer's argument.   **4 A**

5.   Show how the writer's word choice **or** imagery in lines 45–49
    dramatises the 'abortion debate'.   **2 A**

6.   'All Unspeak terms have a shelf life.' (line 50).

    In your own words explain how this idea is developed in lines 50–61.   **2 U**

7.   Read lines 62–70.

    These two paragraphs contain advice from the writer and from
    Orwell on what we can do to combat the deceptive uses of language.
    Which of these paragraphs seems to you to give more vivid expression
    to the advice? Justify your choice by referring to the language of both
    paragraphs.   **4 A/E**

8. Choose one of Didcock's own examples from lines 74–75 and explain why you think it appropriate for inclusion as 'Unspeak'. 　2　U

9. Explain why the writer saves 'repetitive administration of legitimate force' as the example for the final paragraph (lines 76–77). 　1　A

　(28)

Questions on Passage Two

10. Read lines 1–8.

　(a) Identify the differing attitudes to a 'war on terror', one on the part of the military and one on the part of the politicians. 　2　U

　(b) Show how word choice **or** sentence structure in these lines reveals each of these attitudes. 　2　A

11. Read lines 9–22.

　(a) What is ironic about describing teenagers as 'antisocial'? (line 12) 　2　U

　(b) Explain fully why the writer is disturbed by the concept of ASBOs. 　2　U

12. Read lines 23–27.

　Show how imagery in these lines is effective in condemning the misuse of language by politicians. 　2　A

13. Read lines 28–33.

　(a) In your own words explain what is meant by 'pushing a partisan agenda'. 　1　U

　(b) How do the origin and development of the phrase 'ethnic cleansing' illustrate the danger of politically promoted terms? 　2　U

14. 'Purge' was used by Stalin as a euphemism for what was, in fact, a massacre.

　What is any one of the other euphemisms in lines 39–41 designed to disguise? 　1　U

15. (a) Show how sentence structure in lines 42–47 gives impact to Behr's analysis of Steven Poole's views. 　2　A

(b) Do you agree or disagree that the last sentence (lines 49–50) is an effective end to the passage? Briefly justify your answer.   1   E

(17)

Question on both Passages

16. Which writer is more successful in convincing you that the problem of Unspeak is a serious matter? Justify your choice by referring to the **ideas** of both passages.   5   U/E

(5)

Total marks   **(50)**

[END OF QUESTION PAPER]

Paper Five

Christmas

Passage One

In the first passage Madeleine Bunting, in an article published a few days before Christmas, wonders how long the 'traditional' Christmas can survive.

By this point in the run-up to Christmas, most women have a manic look in their eyes. We're hardly capable of intelligible conversation, and those smiles over the mulled wine and mince pies verge on the frantic. If you could peer into our brains, you'd find our synapses working overtime, burning up a
5 power station's worth of mental energy puzzling out what to buy for whom and when.

The two toughest bits of Christmas are thinking what someone would like as a present – and actually finding it. The former is the almost exclusive preserve of women; this is when we're expected to demonstrate those feminine skills
10 of empathy and thoughtfulness. Christmas, for women, is hard emotional labour (with much of the credit going to a mysterious, elusive man).

The blame lies first of all with the Victorians. They pretty much invented Christmas – trees, Santa Claus, puddings, turkeys, decorations, cards, presents, family togetherness – ingeniously turning what had become a sober religious
15 feast into a great festival requiring months of preparation. If women were to be kept at home, they had to have something to do. It had got worse by the middle of the 20th century: the restless housewife not only had her pudding and cake to make, but was fiddling with twigs and silver spray to make table decorations.

20 But the crucial point about the Victorian Christmas, which always gets overlooked, is that it was only the middle classes who had one and it depended on a large amount of servant labour. Now we have the near impossible task of putting on the show single-handed. Add in a hundred or so years of consumer culture and its massive inflation of present
25 expectations, and the formula is designed to produce an epidemic of seasonal migraines and divorces.

Yet the intriguing thing is how we all still struggle to deliver an essentially 19th-century festival. We've never modernised Christmas; the only significant

➤

contribution the 20th century made was TV. It's a great tribute to the
30   Victorians that we still have such a deep attachment to their creation.

It's lasted this long because many of the reasons that made the Victorians
make such a big deal of Christmas are even more in evidence now. The
Victorian rebranding was a response to industrialisation: the family was no
longer the wealth-producing unit; people were swapping work at home for
35   factories and offices; and urbanisation was disrupting the old domestic
structures. Social relations needed strengthening, so the home was relaunched
with rituals such as regular family meals and the Sunday lunch. Home was
idealised as a sanctuary from competitive market capitalism – a place where
vulnerability, innocence, and sentiment could be safely expressed. At the same
40   time, childhood was idealised as a life-stage free of responsibility, a time of
imagination, magic and enchantment. All of this came neatly together in the
rituals the Victorians developed for Christmas.

The tougher the rigours of market capitalism have become, the more fuss
we've made of Christmas. The more fragmented and dispersed families have
45   become, the more the majority of us relish the annual dream of togetherness
(and are bitterly disappointed when it doesn't match up). The harder we
work, the more we want to create the perfect children's Christmas. The more
our children's lives are institutionalised and regimented – in nurseries, in
mugging up for tests – the more we want to give them an experience of
50   magical enchantment. The more we worry about their safety, the more
intensely we want to celebrate innocence; after news of a sickening
child-abduction, we all need Christmas.

It's a form of emotional bulimia. Instead of a year punctuated by festivals, each
with different traditions and all the cause for great eating, drinking and
55   merry-making – as in Catholic Europe and most peasant cultures – Anglo-Saxon
capitalism disciplined the festive impulse into one brief period; presumably, it
ensured factory routine was not disrupted year-round by drunkenness.

The Victorian Christmas, however, is close to breaking point, and it's hard to
see it lasting the 21st century. It was predicated on bored women with little
60   to do, not terminally exhausted working parents. In dual-career families,
Christmas is no longer doable. Hence the escape fantasy: with more women
working and everyone working longer, what people want for Christmas is a
holiday, and they jump at the Sun'n'Santa option from Florida to Thailand.

If I had to make one bet about Christmas ritual in, say, 2043, it would be that
65   very little of it will take place in the home, which will be less a haven than an

➤

outpost of the office. It will no longer be a private family event, but a collective one (of sorts) in hotels, restaurants and resorts. That will ease the bind women are in and will mean an end to rows about washing up; but it will rely on continuing economic inequality to provide the labour to service this
70 kind of Christmas and the cash to buy it.

What will really modernise Christmas is globalisation. Globalisation puts pressure on the routines of the day – the traders who set the alarm to check the Japanese stock market – and on the seasons of the year. The greater the economic integration, the slimmer the chances of a British two-week
75 shutdown holding. Work has already begun to impinge – 37% of fathers will do unscheduled work over Christmas and 22% admit they haven't had time to buy any presents. How much longer can women be relied on to keep the show going?

Passage Two

In the second passage the children's novelist Terence Blacker reflects on the effect Christmas has on the book trade . . . and on families.

'WHAT ARE YOU DOING FOR CHRISTMAS?'

The vast majority of new books published in the UK are sold at Christmas-time: bookshop sales in the last two months of last year were worth £264m (nearly 30 per cent of the £960m total for the year); turnover in December is almost five times what it is in April.

5 But as anyone who writes serious books for a living will know, the two months preceding Christmas, the boom-time for bookshops, are also, by a strange paradox, a disastrous time in which to have a new book published, because the tender shoots of quality fiction, literary biography or sophisticated poetry are invariably crushed underfoot by a bellowing herd of
10 the great TV-reared beasts of the publishing jungle – the glossy cookery books, the semi-literate sporting autobiographies, the TV gardeners and the celebrity explorers – as they stampede towards the check-out tills.

There is something culturally depressing about this trend. It seems to confirm that, as an industry, publishing depends financially on the shifting of books as
15 safe, acceptable objects for giving. A book looks good and feels nice, it tends to flatter the recipient in some way, but the vast majority of those given as

➤

presents will find their way on to the shelf or coffee table or on to the seat beside the loo after no more than a polite glance through their pages.

20 But perhaps here, unusually, the book business is revealing a wider sickness. One does not have to be a miserablist Scrooge to wonder whether the increasing hysteria that surrounds Christmas as a time for giving, for gathering together, for repairing fragile relationships that have been ignored throughout the year, is entirely healthy or sane.

25 We are entering the period in the year when the words 'What are you doing for Christmas?' are to be heard throughout the land. They are rarely spoken with the joy of anticipation. Panicky family plans about how to deal with the problem aunt or the oddball cousin tend to have little to do with love and much to do with a rather dreary form of duty.

30 Maybe it is inevitable. We lead busy, selfish lives. An arrangement that shoe-horns the demands of extended family life into a few fraught, emotional, highly expensive days has brisk contemporary tidiness to it. Under this system, children who have been ignored can be showered with presents, marriages that are drying up can be irrigated with booze, relations who have been forgotten can be appeased with food and fake cheer. It may be tiresome
35 but at least, come January, the duty is over for another year.

No wonder that for so many people, the fortnight at the end of the year is a time not of love or reassurance but of stress and loneliness. Maybe it is time for us to wean ourselves off the excess of the Christmas habit, to try to spread the giving, the time spent with family, the parties, the general bonding of
40 relationships throughout the rest of the year. As in the book trade, more is lost than is gained in placing all one's efforts and expenditure into one brief, feverish moment during the year.

For the truth is that there is one significant economic sector whose business bonanza occurs not in November or December, but in January, after the
45 decorations have come down. Wills are changed, petitions for divorce filed – the Christmas boom-time comes late for our learned friends, the lawyers.

Questions on Passage One

1. Read lines 1–11.

   (a) Why, according to the writer in these lines, is Christmas particularly hard for women?

   2 U

(b) Referring to more than one example, show how the writer creates a light-hearted tone in these lines.   2   A

2. Read lines 12–26.

(a) Show how the writer's word choice in lines 12–19 makes clear her view of the 'Victorian Christmas'.   2   A

(b) Show how the writer's sentence structure in lines 12–19 helps to clarify her view.   2   A

(c) Explain in your own words two factors which, according to lines 20–26, make it more difficult to cope with Christmas now than in Victorian times.   2   U

3. Read lines 27–52.

(a) Explain in your own words what it is that the writer finds 'intriguing'. (line 27)   1   U

(b) Explain in your own words why, according to the writer in lines 31–42, the Victorians made 'such a big deal of Christmas'.   2   U

(c) Why, according to the writer in lines 43–52, is there a desire nowadays for 'the perfect children's Christmas'? (line 47)   2   U

4. How effective do you find the writer's comparison of the way we behave at Christmas to 'emotional bulimia'? (line 53)   3   A/E

5. Read lines 58–70.

(a) Why is the Victorian Christmas 'close to breaking point'? (line 58)   1   U

(b) What does the writer see as an advantage of 'the escape fantasy'? (line 61)   1   U

(c) What disadvantages does she see in it?   2   U

6. Read lines 71–78.

(a) Why, according to the writer, will globalisation 'modernise Christmas'?   2   U

(b) How effective do you find the last sentence of this paragraph as a conclusion to the passage as a whole?   3   E

    (27)

Questions on Passage Two

7. Read lines 1–12.

    (a) By referring to any two examples, show how the writer's
         punctuation in these lines helps to clarify his argument.　　2　A

    (b) Why does the writer think that for 'serious' writers Christmas is
         a 'disastrous time in which to have a new book published'?
         (line 7)　　1　U

    (c) Explain fully how the extended imagery in lines 8–12 makes clear
         the writer's point.　　4　A

8. (a) Why does the writer find the trend he has described in
         paragraphs 1 and 2 'culturally depressing'? (line 13)　　1　U

    (b) Show how the writer creates a dismissive tone in lines 13–18.　　2　A

9. Read lines 19–35.

    (a) Explain in your own words the 'wider sickness' to which the
         writer refers in lines 19–28.　　2　U

    (b) Show how the writer's imagery in lines 29–35 illustrates his
         dissatisfaction with Christmas.　　4　A

10. Read lines 36–46.

    (a) Explain briefly in your own words the writer's solution to the
         problem.　　1　U

    (b) In what way is January a 'boom-time ... for our learned friends,
         the lawyers'?　　1　U

                                                                    (18)

Question on both Passages

11. Which passage, in your opinion, gives a more convincing description
     of the problems and difficulties caused by Christmas?

     Justify your choice by detailed reference to the **ideas** of both passages.　　5　U/E

                                                                    (5)

                                                  Total marks　(50)

[END OF QUESTION PAPER]

Paper Six

Mountains of the Mind

Passage One

The following passage is taken from Mountains of the Mind, *a book by Robert MacFarlane, which considers the contrast between past and present views of mountains and the history and philosophy of mountaineering as a leisure pursuit.*

MOUNTAINS OF THE MIND

Three centuries ago, risking one's life to climb a mountain would have been considered the act of a lunatic. Indeed, the notion barely existed that wild landscape might hold any sort of appeal. To the orthodox seventeenth century imagination, natural scenery was appreciated largely for the extent to which

5 it spoke of agricultural fecundity. Meadows, orchards, grazing fields, the rich ridges of crop lands – these were the ideal components of a landscape. Tamed landscapes, in other words, were attractive: landscapes which had had a human order imposed on them by the plough, the hedgerow and the ditch. Mountains, nature's roughest productions, were not only agriculturally

10 intractable, they were also aesthetically repellent: it was felt that their irregular and gargantuan outlines upset the natural spirit level of the mind.

Moreover, mountains were dangerous places to be. It was believed that avalanches could be triggered by stimuli as light as a cough, the foot of a beetle, or the brush of a bird's wing as it swooped low across a loaded snow

15 slope. You might fall between the blue jaws of a crevasse, to be regurgitated years later by the glacier, pulped and rigid. True, mountains had in the past provided refuge for beleaguered people but for the most part they were a form of landscape to be avoided. Go around mountains by all means, it was thought, or travel along their flanks or go between them if absolutely

20 necessary – as many merchants, soldiers, pilgrims and missionaries had to – but certainly not up them.

During the second half of the 1700s, however, people started for the first time to travel to mountains out of a spirit other than necessity, and a coherent sense began to develop of the splendour of mountainous landscape. The

25 summit of Mont Blanc was reached in 1786, and mountaineering proper came into existence in the middle of the 1800s, stimulated by a commitment to science (in the sport's adolescence, no respectable mountaineer would scale

➤

a peak without at the very least boiling a thermometer on the summit) but
very definitely born of beauty. The complex aesthetics of ice, sunlight, rock,
30 height, angles and air were unquestionably marvellous. Mountains began to
exert a considerable and often fatal power of attraction on the human mind.
The year the Matterhorn was climbed for the first time, four of the successful
summiteers fell to their deaths during the descent.

Today, the emotions and attitudes which impelled the early mountaineers still
35 prosper in the Western imagination; indeed if anything they are more
unshiftably settled there. Mountain-worship is a given to millions of people.
The vertical, the ferocious, the icy – all these are now automatically revered
forms of landscape, images of which permeate an urbanised Western culture
increasingly hungry for even second-hand experiences of wildness and
40 wilderness. Mountain going has been one of the fastest growing leisure
activities of the past twenty years. An estimated 10 million Americans go
mountaineering annually, and 50 million go hiking. Some 4 million people in
Britain consider themselves to be hill-walkers of one kind or another. Global
sales of outdoor products and services are reckoned at 10 billion dollars
45 annually, and growing.

Over the course of three centuries, therefore, a tremendous revolution of
perception occurred in the West concerning mountains. The qualities for
which mountains were once reviled – steepness, desolation, perilousness –
came to be numbered among their most prized aspects.

50 So drastic was this revolution that to contemplate it now is to be reminded of
a truth about landscapes: that our responses to them are for the most part
culturally devised. That is to say, when we look at a landscape, we do not see
what is there, but largely what we think is there. We attribute qualities to a
landscape which it does not intrinsically possess – savageness, for example, or
55 bleakness – and we value it accordingly. For centuries mountains were
regarded as useless obstructions. Now they are numbered among the natural
world's most exquisite forms, and people are willing to die for love of them.

What we call a mountain is thus in fact a collaboration between the real
physical geology of the world and the imagination of humans – a mountain of
60 the mind. And the way people behave towards mountains has little or nothing
to do with the actual objects of rock and ice themselves. Mountains are only
contingencies of geology. They do not kill deliberately; nor do they
deliberately please: any emotional properties which they possess are imposed
on them by human imaginations. Mountains – like deserts, polar tundra, deep
65 oceans, jungles and all the other wild landscapes that we have romanticised –

➢

are simply there, and there they remain, their physical structures rearranged gradually over time by the forces of geology and weather. They exist over and beyond human perceptions of them. But they are also the products of human perceptions; they have been *imagined* into existence down the centuries.

70 A disjunction between the imagined and the real is a characteristic of all human activities, and it finds one of its sharpest expressions in the mountains. Stone, rock and ice are significantly less amenable to the hand's touch than to the mind's eye, and the mountains of the earth have often turned out to be more resistant, more fatally real, than the mountains of the mind. The 75 mountains one gazes at, reads about, dreams of and desires are not the mountains one climbs. The latter are matters of hard, steep, sharp rock and freezing snow; of extreme cold; of a vertigo so physical it can cramp your stomach and loosen your bowels; of hypertension, nausea and frostbite. And of unspeakable beauty.

Passage Two

The following passage by the poet and novelist Andrew Greig tells of his preparation for going on a Himalayan mountaineering expedition in his capacity as a writer/recorder of the expedition. As he had previously almost no experience of climbing mountains he had to cram in as much climbing as possible before the expedition departed from Scotland.

SUMMIT FEVER

To call mountaineering a sport or a pastime is like calling monastic life a hobby. For those who become serious about it, it is the core of their lives. Everything else is arranged around it. It affects their attitude to everything else.

5 As the time went by I gradually exchanged one obsession, writing, for another, climbing – though I denied and derided it to the last. I picked up the elements of 'Good Brit Style': not to be seen training, not to have gleaming new gear, to play down all but one's fears and fiascos. To drink too much too late, to get up reluctantly and late next morning, moaning and groaning, to arrive at the foot 10 of the route with three hours' daylight left *and still climb it:* that was considered Good Style. I had little problem in acquiring that.

The style was one thing, the substance another. Due to poor weather I only had another four weekends' winter climbing in Glencoe. Yet the promise and

➤

threat of these changed my entire winter, made it something to be enjoyed
15   rather than just suffered. Weekdays were a time for recovery and appreciation
of home comforts, with the weekend to both dread and anticipate. My social
life was suddenly full of climbers, climbing talk, climbing plans and
reminiscences. Much laughter, abuse, and friendship, shared experience.
And gradually, the beginning of composure.

20   It was, quite simply, very exciting; it dramatized my life.

By the end of the season, I'd done a grand total of six Scottish routes, none
particularly testing, and an amount of yomping about on the hills. It was an
absurdly inadequate background for going to the Himalayas – the norm would
be several Scottish winters, then a few seasons in the Alps doing classics and
25   adding some new routes, and only then might one consider the Himalayas.

And some days during my preparation I had no appetite or nerve for it at all,
when climbing was all slog and fear and trembling and wanting it to be over
with, hating it. But other days. . .

One day in particular remains with me, always will. A day when nervousness
30   took the form of controlled energy, when I wanted to climb, when I had the
appetite. Then I rejoiced in the challenge of the crux of the climb; pulling up
and over it and moving on; I was lifted up like a surfer on a great wave of
adrenalin. The day was perfect: ice blue, ice cold, needle-bright. After two
hours in the shadowed gully I finally pulled myself though the notch in the
35   cornice overhanging the top, and in my eyes was a dazzling world of sunlight
and gleaming ridges and all the summits of Glencoe clear across to Ben Nevis.
My companion silhouetted against the sun; a few climbers moving on the
summit ridge; my panting exhilaration – in that moment I felt like a king, and
what I saw in front of me was the earth as Paradise, blue, golden and white,
40   dazzlingly pure.

The intensity we win through effort! In that pristine clarity of the air and the
senses, the simplest experiences become almost mystical in their intensity. A
cigarette smoked in the lee of a cairn; an orange segment squirting in the
mouth and the smell of it filling the moment, making the world fruit; the patch
45   of lichen inches from your face; the final pulling off of boots at the end of the
day – Glencoe and winter climbing gave me moments of completeness. I will
never forget them.

Questions on Passage One

1. Read lines 1–11.

   (a) What kind of landscape appealed to the seventeenth century imagination?   **1   U**

   (b) By referring to two examples from these lines, show how word choice used to describe this landscape demonstrates its appeal to the people of the time.   **2   A**

2. Referring to lines 12–16 ('...rigid'), show how the two dangers associated with mountains are highlighted by the imagery the writer uses to describe each.   **4   A**

3. Show how the sentence 'During the second half ... splendour of a mountainous landscape' (lines 22–24) acts as a link in the writer's line of thought. You should refer to specific words and phrases from the sentence in your answer.   **2   U**

4. *(a)* Read lines 34–40 ('...wilderness').
   Explain in your own words why the attraction of mountains is important to 'urbanised Western culture'.   **2   U**

   (b) What two main pieces of evidence are presented in the remainder of this paragraph (lines 40–45) to prove the popularity of mountain going?   **2   U**

5. Read lines 46–49.

   Show how this paragraph fulfils an important function in the structure of the passage up to this point.   **2   A**

6. *(a)* Read lines 50–57.
   What is the meaning of the phrase 'culturally devised' (line 52)?   **1   U**

   (b) How does the content of the remainder of the paragraph from 'That is to say...' (line 52) expand on this idea?   **2   U**

7. Read lines 58–69.

   (a) 'Mountains are only contingencies of geology.' (lines 61–62) In your own words explain the meaning of this sentence and show how the meaning is clarified by any one of the statements which follow it.   **2 U**

   (b) Show how sentence structure in these lines helps to clarify the explanation.   **2 A**

8. How does the language of the final paragraph (lines 70–79) bring out the contrast between the imagined and the real experience of mountains? You may wish to consider such features as sentence structure, word choice, imagery, sound...   **4 A**

       (26)

Questions on Passage Two

9. How effective is the simile in lines 1–2 in showing the writer's fascination with mountaineering?   **2 A/E**

10. *(a)* What does the description of 'Good Brit Style' in lines 5–11 reveal about his and his friends' attitude to mountaineering?   **2 U**

    (b) Show how the writer's sentence structure in these lines adds to the impact of his description of 'Good Brit Style'.   **2 A**

11. 'It was, quite simply, very exciting; it dramatised my life.' (line 20)

    Show how the sentence structure in lines 12–19 demonstrates the excitement or the drama of his experience.   **2 A**

12. By referring to lines 21–25, explain why he felt unprepared for climbing in the Himalayas.   **2 U**

13. Show how the imagery of lines 29–40 highlights the positive aspects of climbing on the particular day he is describing. You should consider at least two images.   **4 A**

14. 'The intensity we win through effort!' (line 41)

    (a) Explain what the writer means by this.   **1 U**

    (b) Show how word choice and sentence structure in lines 41–47 illustrate the intensity of the experience.   **4 A**

    (19)

Question on Both Passages

15. Which passage do you feel creates more interest in the subject of mountaineering? By examining the **ideas and** the **style** of both passages justify your choice. In your discussion of style you might consider such features as tone, structure, imagery...   5   E

(5)

Total marks   (50)

[END OF QUESTION PAPER]